MAR 22

BE THE LEADER YOUR
TEAM DESERVES —

I AM A LEADER
MY TEAM PLAYS TO WIN!

Task Force 2-4 Cav - "First In, Last Out": The History of the 2d Squadron, 4th Cavalry Regiment, During Operation Desert Storm

25th Anniversary Edition

by
Joseph C. Barto III

With Forward by
Coach Mike Krzyzewski
Duke University Head Basketball Coach

Task Force 2-4 Cav - "First In, Last Out" : The History of the 2d Squadron, 4th Cavalry Regiment, During Operation Desert Storm / by Joseph C. Barto III.

First Printing: 1993 U.S. Army Command and General Staff College
Second Printing: 25th Anniversary Edition 2018 by Joseph C. Barto III

Library of Congress Cataloging-in-Publication Data

ISBN <978-1-387-71442-1>

Book published through and available from Lulu.com website.

Includes bibliographical references (p. 139).

1. United States. Army. Infantry Division (Mechanized), 24th-History-20th century.

2. Persian Gulf War, 1991-Regimental histories-United States.

3. United States. Army-History-Persian Gulf War, 1991.

FOREWORD

Welcome to the 25th Anniversary Edition of TF 2-4 CAV First In – Last Out. During Operation Desert Storm when Joe was leading his TF 2-4 CAV Team to win in early 1991; I was leading my Duke team to our first National Championship. Both were significant events of our lives.

Joe and I both published books telling the story of these events. In 1993 both his _TF 2-4 CAV: First In – Last Out_ and my _A Season Is a Lifetime_ were published shortly after the actual events. They were more about "What" happened during those brief periods of time. 25th Anniversary editions are unique because they add the perspective of time about the impact of "What" we did. Time passing makes the meaning of those events much more about "Who" we did it with than "What" we did. Maybe most importantly, the theme is "How" it affected the rest of our lives. Over the years the detail of "What" we did seem to fade while the power of "Who" we did it with and how it shaped the rest of our lives continues to deepen and grow.

I first met Joe in the Spring of 1973 while he was a High School Senior and I was Coaching at the USMA Prep School recruiting him to West Point. Our Prep School team there went 20-1…high performing. While our few years together were brief, it also shaped both of our futures. We learned a lot together. I know if I had not had those 5 years at West Point; I would never have been so successful at Duke and I know if Joe had not had his 4 years at West Point and as an Army basketball player, he would never have been so successful in his career as an Army Officer, business leader, husband, and father. We are, at the end of the day, West Point graduates who were privileged to lead in so many ways. I learned at West Point that failure is not a destination, don't try to do it by yourself, and being responsible for the performance of a group of people on a noble mission is the greatest gift of our lives. It has been my honor and privilege to lead and I am truly blessed to have had a lifetime of leading high performing teams. I know Joe shares that commitment and dedication. We know Leaders never get to have a bad day.

As you read the story of TF 2-4 CAV, I know you will sense the same passion, love of his soldiers, and a total focus on accomplishing the mission while bringing his soldiers home with their heads held high. Joe completely understands it is not only accomplishing the mission but serving with honor and being proud of how they did their incredibly successful work together.

This is what sets a 25th Anniversary edition apart. It is about how we led, the impact on the rest of our lives, and who we did it with. To the troopers of TF 2-4 CAV; Congratulations and Job Well Done. When your country called on you; you did your duty and this book tells your story. Now the 25th Anniversary edition provided you the chance to complete the story with how it affected the rest of your lives and this is why America is so great.

Coach Mike Krzyzewski
Duke University Men's Basketball
USMA 1969
Durham, NC

AUTHOR'S FOREWORD

In 1993 when we first published the book, I had four objectives. The book had to be free, short, and tell both the military facts of our units operations and how it <u>felt</u> to be a recent graduate of the Command and General Staff College, who went to war and served as a Major on a Division staff and then as a Cavalry Squadron Executive Officer that led soldiers in combat.

In the Fall of 2015, CSM (Retired) Jean Soucy asked if I was going to attend the 24th Infantry Division (Mechanized) Association's Operation Desert Shield/Storm 25th Anniversary Reunion at Fort Stewart. I had no idea there was a 24ID(M) Association or that they had been holding reunions over the years. For the 25th Anniversary, our Operation Desert Shield and Storm Commanding General, General Barry R. McCaffrey, led the official party and delivered the keynote at the spot we dedicated the Memorial to our fallen comrades on the first anniversary in 1992.

Jean and I had stayed in touch over the years since, and I was excited to accept his invitation to join him in representing the Task Force at the reunion. I have a tremendous loyalty and allegiance to our CSM who was such an enormous support to me and the Task Force (TF). Jean had arranged a dinner the evening before the reunion for the TF 2-4 CAV veterans in attendance to kick off our weekend together. While I was very excited to see old friends and comrades; there were also a list of names I did not recognize and I wondered how this would go.

On the appointed day, Jean and I met at the bar prior to dinner to conduct a "*Rock Drill*" in true Cavalry fashion. I had not actually seen him since 1992 when I had departed Fort Stewart. The emotion from first sight was overwhelming and quite unexpected.

As the unit gathered you could feel the emotions growing. The A Troop contingent was led by the Troop Commander, Dave Gallup and 1SG Chuck Hill. We went around the table and introduced ourselves; Barto, Squadron Executive Officer; Soucy, Command Sergeant Major; Edwards, Commander Task Force Air Cav; Dan Payne Squadron Chaplain, and then it was Rob Davis and his wife Donna, Driver A35; Jerry Moore, Driver A12, and Tim Montgomery Driver A33. Most attendees, many with their wives, had been 19-20 year-old Privates and Specialists on their first and last tours in the Army. They had traveled from all over the county to remember their historic service together in late 1990 and early 1991 during Operations Desert Shield and Storm as members of Task Force 2-4 CAV.

I was stunned by the depth of the emotion we all felt around that table. In the acknowledgments of the 1993 version I wrote; "*War is an intensely emotional event. There is a special bond between the leaders and the led when based upon trust, confidence, and love. It is a special love that is difficult to describe yet easy to identify—you can see it in their eyes when they meet and hear it in their voices when they talk about what they have done.*"

Sitting next to Rob Davis at dinner, I was telling him my story of working in Division G-3 Operations and how I became the Squadron XO, how we had put the plan together, and all the SXO war stories. I then asked him what he thought; he looked at me and said, "Sir, I was just the driver of A35... my view of the war was whatever my Bradley Commander, SSG McNeary told me to do... my war was about staying dry, keeping my Bradley running, and taking care of my crew mates. No idea what you are talking about." with a huge smile.

I flashed back to my Dad, Joseph C. Barto, Jr., a World War II veteran of the 704 Tank Destroyer Battalion, 4th Armored Division from Utah Beach to Victory in Europe Day doing a History Channel

**TF 2-4 CAV Operation Desert Storm 25th Anniversary Dinner
February 21, 2016 Savannah, Georgia**

Bottom Row (left–right) Jerry Houpt Driver A15, Tim Montgomery Driver A33, Dave Salenbien Driver A32, CSM Jean Soucy, Rob Davis Driver A35, 1st Sgt Hill

2nd Row – Tracey Ference Loader/Observer A11, Edward Donnelly Gunner A33, Dewayne Sims Driver A65, Joe Barto Squadron XO, Dan Payne Squadron Chaplain, Clay Edwards TF Air Cav Commander, Tim Cox Gunner A65, Dave Gallop, A Troop Commander.

Back Row – Jerry Moore Driver A12, Stuart Mica Driver A34

WWII interview in the 1990's. When asked what he thought of General Patton's plan for the famous Thunder Run to break the siege at Bastogne in December 1944. *"No idea what you are talking about; all I remember I was driving a Tank Destroyer north for 28 hours and it was coldest I have ever been in my life."* American soldiers all share a common bond depending on where they were, what their roles were, and who they were with.

As dinner and drinks continued through the evening, I noticed that many had the book *"TF 2-4 CAV First In—Last Out"* and as they would talk about some event they would refer to the book then *"do you remember that day ..."*. I was so pleased, because this is why I wrote the book ... to record the events of our time together just for this specific reason ... a common chronology of the events of our war. There were several versions of the book present. After dinner, one of the troopers came up to me to thank me for writing the book and how special it was to them and their family. I assured him it was no big deal and I was very happy it served its objectives when he said *"Sir, you don't get it do you? You told OUR story. None of these other units have a book that tells their story."*

Over the weekend and weeks following, I had more requests on how to get a copy of the book, which had been out of print for many years. Thus, the idea to publish this 25th Anniversary Edition for those troopers who as General Patton once said, *"could put their grandchildren on their knees for the rest of their lives and tell their war story"* of the events surrounding Task Force 2-4 CAV during Operations Desert Shield and Storm.

A Troop First Sergeant Chuck Hill, Squadron Command Sergeant Major Jean Soucy, Squadron Executive Officer Joe Barto, and A Troop Commander Dave Gallup

That conversation with Rob Davis began the 25th Anniversary edition process. It is all about where you were and your perspective, which is why we decided to re-publish. Our goal is for every trooper and their families for generations to come to be able to pull this book off the shelf and tell their story. Often, that story has little to do with what happened during the 100-hour war, it is about leaving home and their families at home, listening to *"God Bless the USA"* 1,000 times in the hangar at Hunter Army Airfield waiting for an airplane, getting off an airplane in Dammam, Saudi Arabia in 120 degrees in August and riding in their Bradley Fighting Vehicle on the back of a Heavy Equipment Trailer driver by a non-English speaking local national and being dropped off in the middle of the desert and wondering *"What do we do now?"*. It is a talent show over Thanksgiving; it is when a buddy helps you, and you he, for no reason. It is your first call home after being gone for three months. It goes on and on and on.

40 Days. My first day at TF 2-4 CAV was February 2, 1991, we attacked into Iraq on February 22 and on March 14, 1991 we crossed the border back into Saudi Arabia. Sometimes you only get one chance to get it right.

The Road Home. March 17, 1991. Outside of Dammam, Saudi Arabia. 1LT John Roddy, A Troop Executive Officer; Major Joe Barto, Squadron Executive Officer; Specialist Raymond Green, my driver and Battle Buddy

What if … I had not gone on that 1973 basketball recruiting visit to West Point followed by a stop at the USMA Prep School in Fort Belvoir, Virginia, where I met a young Army Captain and Basketball Coach named Mike Krzyzewski and had not answered the phone a week later. Coach told me that if I chose to come the Prep School, play basketball for him and go to West Point, it would be the "*best decision of my life.*" When for the next five years, I often thought it was the worst decision of my life.

Army Basketball Team 1975-1976
Left Standing: Coach Mike Krzyzewski; Joe Barto #34

What if … Coach K had not put me, a rarely played reserve, in the biggest game of the 1975-76 season against Florida State at the University of Vermont Holiday Tournament, where I embarrassed myself, my team, and my family with the worst display of basketball ever. Soon afterwards Coach and I deciding leaving the team would be best for me and the team.

I would have never made the Dean's list for the next two semesters and improved my class rank high enough to choose to be an Armor officer (108 out of 120 available spaces). I went to West Point to play basketball but fell in love with being an Army officer and leader. I was born to be a soldier and to lead. I may have never had the chance to lead soldiers in combat and tell their story.

What if ... I never attended the induction of Coach K into the Army Basketball Hall of Fame in 1995 at West Point and thanked him for putting me in that game in 1975 because I was not ready to play on that day but that lesson learned ensured that on February 1, 1990, when then MG McCaffrey put me in the biggest game of my life, I was ready. When I asked Coach Krzyzewski why he put me in that game, he immediately remembered the event and while I believed he had some vindictive intent for me personally he said, *"The only reason I put you in that game is because I thought you could help us Win. The problem was you didn't believe you could."*

Coach says the secret of life, *"... is aligning yourself with people who believe in you more than you believe in yourself."* When I walked into the TF 2-4 CAV TOC for the first time on February 2, 1991, I knew my first mission was to believe in them because they did not believe in themselves that day. To do that, I had to believe in myself before they would believe in me creating that sacred bond between the leader and the led.

What if ... I had not been at the intersection of Vessey and West St. in New York City at 8:46 AM on September 11, 2001, when I saw the fireball of the first plane hitting the north tower through the sunroof of the car I was sitting in and had not made the decision that it was time to do something bold in my life. I decided that I could either work for companies who made decisions for me, my team and my family or if I was going to take a bet on myself.

My mission in life since July 2002 is to help others know what it feels like to be on a high-performance team who seek perfection every day, just like we did in TF 2-4 CAV. The officers and troopers of TF 2-4 CAV knew they had one chance to get this perfect; one hour, one day, one mission at a time. Certainly, every action was not perfect but we accomplished our mission and returned home with their head held high. PERFECT. Mission First – People Always!

What if ... I had not walked into the Mademoiselle Dress Shop in Annandale, Virginia in April 1977 and met Tricia O'Donnell—she and I have always believed in each other more than we could ever believe in ourselves. An African proverb says, *"If you want to go fast; go alone. If you want to go far; go together."* We have had an amazing journey together, with a long way to go. She is the leader of our family and leads by example with such great courage and commitment.

When I work with teams today and, usually near the end of our time together, I hand them a small piece of paper and ask them to write down the name of the person in their lives that believed in them more than they believed in themselves. Who was that person or persons who changed their lives? I encourage them to remember what it felt like to be around them and how they affected their lives. Then I ask them to turn that slip of paper over and write down the name of the person who would write their name down on the front.

For 40 days plus 25 years, I am privileged to have leaders and led from TF 2-4 CAV on both sides of the slip of paper I always carry in my wallet.

In closing, I have one very late but very important correction to make for Rob Davis, Driver A35 during our dinner conversation. Rob Davis was not **"JUST"** the driver of A35; Rob Davis was **"THE"** driver of A35 just as my father was not "JUST" the mechanic/driver of a 704th Tank Destroyer. Nor was Jerry Houpt Driver A15, Tim Montgomery Driver A33, Dave Salenbien Driver A32, Tracey Ference Loader/Observer A11, Edward Donnelly Gunner A33, Dewayne Sims Driver A65, Tim Cox Gunner A65, Jerry Moore Driver A12, Stuart Mica Driver A34 or any of the men and women who did fulfill their sole responsibilities to the team no matter what the role.

The reason for this 25th Anniversary edition and the core of the American Army is fact that **"THE"** Driver of A35 was part of the A35 TEAM, A35 was part of the 3rd Platoon TEAM, part of the A Troop TEAM, part of the TF 2-4 CAV TEAM, part of the 24 ID(M) TEAM, the XVIII Airborne Corps TEAM, the Central Command TEAM, and ultimately the American Army TEAM who chose to do their duty, be a part of the greatest military TEAM in the history of the world, and were proud and honored by the American people to be given the chance to serve. It begins and ends with the American soldier; accomplishing the mission and returning home with their heads held high, proud of what they and their TEAM have done.

Prepared and Loyal!

A25 Crew
Bradley Commander: SSG Arredondo
Gunner: SPC Chris Dallas
Driver: SPC Chris [unknown last name]
Assistant Gunner/Dismount: SPC Robert West
Loader/Dismount: SPC Anthony "Grave Digger" Jones

3rd Platoon: Platoon Leader LT David Halcolm, Platoon Sergeant SFC Walter Bell; SSG Nesbitt A Section Sec Sgt (A32), SGT Hernandez Squad Leader (A33 BC), SFC. Steve McNeary B Section Sec Sgt. (A35), William DeJesus Squad Leader (A36 BC).

25th Anniversary Edition
CONTENTS

25th Anniversary Edition

ILLUSTRATIONS & TABLES

Figures

Maps

Tables

25th Anniversary Edition

PREFACE

I compiled the large majority of the facts and details included in this paper during Operation Desert Storm, through my personal observation. I kept a journal of the events as they happened and updated them several times after significant events. Since my battle position was as the squadron executive officer and the officer in charge of the tactical operations center (TOC), I was intimately involved in the planning and execution of every event in the task force from the moment of my arrival at the TOC on the morning of 2 February 1991 through the redeployment of the squadron to Fort Stewart on 23 March 1991.

As the executive officer, I attended all of the division planning events with the squadron commander and took detailed notes, which I have used as source documents. Immediately following the cease-fire, I took several hours to go over my notes and transcribe, to the best of my then-fresh recollection, the events as they actually occurred in the task force TOC and as they were reported in the detailed reports submitted to the TOC from the troops and companies assigned to the task force and in communications with higher headquarters.

Additionally, on 5 March 1991, the task force conducted its immediate after-action review at the task force TOC located forty kilometers west of Basra (Basrah), Iraq, where I acted as primary recorder. The entire leadership of the task force was present at this meeting, with the exception of the S3 who had already redeployed to the United States. Otherwise, all of the command group, commanders, and staff were present, and an in-depth discussion of events, tactics, techniques, and procedures occurred.

The operations of the air cavalry troops are not discussed in this work except when they were actually under the operational control of the task force. While these soldiers did yeoman's work, I was not directly involved in their activities and have little firsthand knowledge of their activities. Thus, I have intentionally not included their exploits and significant contributions to the success of the division.

Since returning from Southwest Asia and reading other histories, I have found some differences in times and events in the division and various brigade accounts of the war. After investigation and using a little common sense, I discovered that in a 25,000-soldier division combat team, not everyone does the same things at the same time. Also, because the task force was not able to be in continuous communication with the division command and control nodes, the task force sometimes got division orders several hours after they were issued-an example of what is called the "fog of war."

Prior to my assignment to the task force, I was a watch officer and then chief of G3 Operations at the division main command post. My primary responsibilities were to write the division's fragmentary orders, draft the daily division commander's situation report, and brief the division command group at the nightly division commander's update. These duties required an intimate knowledge of all the operations throughout the division. Therefore, the activities and current operational situation of TF 2-4 Cav were familiar to me from the alert on 7 August 1990 through my arrival at the task force TOC on 2 February 1991.

Obviously, I could not know everything about its operations; therefore, over the course of the past year, I have interviewed every key player in the task force (most of whom have read the several drafts of this paper). Their comments and insights have been graciously included where appropriate. I confess that many of these interviews were not of the formal sort but occurred over camp stoves and MRE's at some training area at Fort Stewart, as old comrades in arms relived the various events of the war. I was very careful, however, to find and interview those soldiers who were at the scene during the key events of the operation. Also, I credit Major Jason K. Kamiya for his work, A History of the 24th Mechanized Infantry Division Combat Team During Operation Desert Storm. I have used his work extensively to confirm the divisional operations as they applied to the task force.

While some may not agree with all of the facts and assertions of this work, I have been careful not to confuse my work and Kamiya's. Everything included in this document is true to the best of my knowledge. The events of Operation Desert Storm as I have detailed them here are the reality as I perceived it and I was intimately involved with the events.

I would be remiss if I did not acknowledge the significant part my comrades' recollections and contributions played in completing my work. I constantly badgered Lieutenant Colonel Tom Leney, Major Lou Gelling, Captain Pete Utley, and Command Sergeant Major Jean Soucy to verify events, and they always had time for me. First Lieutenant Brian Hann worked his magic by producing those diagrams and figures in this work. There is a long list of names of others who were instrumental to this effort, but they are too numerous to name, so I will not make the attempt.

The most difficult professional task I have ever accomplished was to stand in front of the forty-five soldiers assigned to the TOC on the morning of 23 February 1991 and communicate to them the confidence and knowledge that we could and would accomplish the mission and come home alive with our heads held high. I was personally and specifically responsible for these fine young men during the ground war, and I felt the burden of this sacred responsibility. Even though we were together for only a short period, we had become brothers, and I owe my entire experience to them. On that momentous day, I explained the entire plan to them one more time and ended my talk with, "*All I ask is that you give me ten days of stone cold soldiering and we will be all right.*" They did and we were. Even though they are in far-flung places now, we will always be bonded through that special brotherhood of war. There are four people I must acknowledge specifically: Master Sergeant (P) Bernard Cabrerra, Staff Sergeant James Gill, Specialist George "The General" Jenkins, and my driver and battle buddy, Specialist Raymond Green.

25th Anniversary Edition

25th Anniversary Edition

ACKNOWLEDGMENTS

Love and fear are two of man's most intense emotions. During Operations Desert Shield and Desert Storm, I learned fear is usually directly proportional to one's situational awareness; love for your wife, family, friends, and soldiers is distinctly different but often equally as intense.

During Operation Desert Storm, I never experienced fear, either because I knew the enemy and friendly situation, did not know enough to be scared, or was too tired and busy to care. The soldiers' families, separated by thousands of miles and the unknown, were those who knew raw fear, and they stared it down every day. They were the true heroes and heroines of Operation Desert Storm. My wife, Tricia, and my three sons, Joey, Tommy, and Kevin, survived the truly incredible task of daily life when love and fear were constantly tugging at their hearts and souls. Tricia and I owe a special debt of gratitude to those extraordinary family and friends who shared the love and fear with compassion and empathy during the most intense emotional times of our lives.

On Christmas Eve 1990, a Catholic priest said one of twenty-seven masses over a three-day period at the main command post of the 24th Infantry Division (Mechanized). His Christmas message was short. He challenged us to remember the last five Christmases. Who was there? What happened? What gifts were given or received? While desperately searching the recesses of our minds for those elusive details, he gently suggested that as homesick as we felt, this Christmas would always be remembered in every detail. He closed with the notion that Christmas represents a new beginning. My life will always be divided into two distinct periods separated by the defense of Saudi Arabia and the liberation of Kuwait. My new beginning started on 23 March 1991 when my two-year-old son, Kevin, broke through the crowd, dodged the military policemen and ran into my arms.

But this publication is not about me. It is for and about the soldiers of Task Force 2-4 Cav. My personal account is not special, or even noteworthy, but merely represents the thoughts, feelings, and experiences of any soldier who answered the call, served, overcame the fear, and upheld the honorable warrior ethic of the profession of arms by doing his duty in a heroic, yet curiously ordinary, fashion. Task Force 2-4 Cav left Iraq on 14 March and on 22 March 1993 boarded an airplane homeward bound. In the ensuing melee of post-combat operations, reconstitution, leave, parades, and general euphoria, the events of Operation Desert Storm began to fade or take on a life of their own. This project began as a simple recording of the facts that surrounded our participation in Operation Desert Storm.

Somewhere in the midst of that simple process, and due largely to the encouragement of Dr. Sam Lewis, Major Dan Bolger, and Major Joe Martz, the writing became more than simply a record, it turned into a saga. The momentum of my ideas increased as the memories faded and the families, friends, and soldiers wanted to either know or remember what happened during the early months of 1991 in Saudi Arabia and Iraq. This saga is recorded principally for them.

War is an intensely emotional event. There is a special bond between leaders and the led, which is based upon trust, confidence, and love. It is a special love that is difficult to describe yet easy to identify. You can see it in their eyes when they meet and hear it in their voices when they talk about what they have done.

I am honored to be part of their brotherhood and privileged to tell their story. This narrative is dedicated to all who shared the love and the fear.

March 13, 2018

Thanks...

In 2017 due to the power of the internet, Bill McCowen reached out to re-connect with me after 30+ years. I was Bill's Company Commander in C Company, 3rd Battalion, 1st Armor Training Brigade at Fort Knox, Kentucky in 1980-81. Every 13 weeks C-3-1 turned 200 or so young American new recruits into soldiers and M60-A3 tank crewman. In every class, certain trainees stood out and Bill was along the most outstanding of those. In fact, he was recommended by his Drill Sergeant to be a Tank Commander "Hold Over" which was a program where the best trainees were selected to remain for an additional training cycle to now teach to the next group what they had just learned. Bill excelled in this role and when he left for assignment to the "infamous" 13th Tank in Germany, he continued his own outstanding military career and life afterwards. When he graduated a second time, it was the last time we had contact until I received his email; subject line "Tankers by God".

During a follow-up re-connect call he asked if he could get a copy of the book. In typical Armored Cavalryman fashion when I told him that the book was out of print he responded with "well let's fix that." I don't know if he had any idea what he had signed he and his wife Tambra up for. I may have been his leader in C-3-1 but he and Tambra become my leader since then as they did the lion's share of the work to edit, coordinate, create the website, and ultimately coordination for the publication of the book you now hold. There is no way for me to express my gratitude and thanks for their professionalism, dedication, and love that they put into this project. I am forever grateful.

Bill and Tambra — "Well done, my true and faithful brother and sister in arms — well done!" This is another example of the best of being a member of the United States Army and we may thank God for our chance to serve others and the bonds we make.

I. INTRODUCTION

On the beautiful spring day of 23 March 1991, excitement filled the air as the families of the 2d Squadron, 4th Cavalry Regiment (2-4 Cav), filled the Cottrell Field stands at Fort Stewart, Georgia. The loudspeaker boomed patriotic music and the announcer ended the countdown that had begun more than seven months earlier with, "*Your heroes are home!*" The bannered buses pulled into the parking lot and disgorged the weary troopers a mere 100 meters from the gym where many of them were manifested for deployment the previous August.

The wives, sons, daughters, mothers, fathers, sisters, and brothers waited breathlessly in a carnival atmosphere as the long journey for these courageous soldiers and families was about to end. The command sergeant major formed the squadron and unfurled the colors. The squadron commander gave the command to cross those final 100 meters, thus ending another epic drama in the proud history of the 4th Cavalry Regiment.

This chapter in the regiment's history continued a tradition begun before the Civil War. In August 1860, the 1st United States Cavalry Regiment, which had been formed in 1855 at Fort Leavenworth, Kansas, was re-designated the 4th Cavalry Regiment and posted to the American West to protect the early settlers and to maintain law and order on the frontier.

Upon completion of organization, the regiment was ordered to Fort Riley, Kansas, under the command of Colonel Edwin V. Sumner. Among the officers posted to the regiment were such notables as Lieutenant Colonel Joseph E. Johnston, Major John Sedgwick, Major William Emory, Captain J. E. B. Stuart, and Captain George B. McClellan. All these officers, except Johnston and Stuart, remained loyal at the beginning of the Civil War. Proud of their loyalty, the regiment adopted the motto, Prepared and Loyal. The regiment participated in twenty Civil War campaigns.[1]

After the war, the 4th Cavalry returned to frontier duty before being sent to the Philippines from 1898-1907, which added another ten battle streamers to its regimental colors and established its tradition of worldwide deployment. During World War II, the regiment boasted that it landed the first four troopers on the shores at

Normandy; thus, five more campaign streamers were added to its colors. The 4th Cavalry then saw action in Korea and Vietnam, while the 2d Squadron was assigned to the 1st and then the 4th Armored Divisions in Germany.

In July 1972, the 2d Squadron was deactivated and then was reactivated in January 1987 at Fort Stewart, Georgia, as the divisional cavalry squadron of the 24th Infantry Division (Mechanized) (Victory Division). During Operation Desert Storm in the Persian Gulf, the 1st Squadron of the regiment also saw action with the 1st Infantry Division (Mechanized).[2]

The purpose of this work is threefold. The first is to record the actions of Task Force (TF) 2-4 Cav during Operation Desert Storm. The second is to establish a framework for future study using this task force as an example. Through the experiences of TF 2-4 Cav in the Persian Gulf, many lessons can be learned in the areas of training, organization, leadership, doctrine, logistics, and the quality of the American soldier. Finally, I add my comments and experiences of the operation so the reader can develop an understanding of the personal nature of war. Through-out this work, my personal comments are in italics.

At the same time, my detailed discussion of the plan, its execution, and the organizational environment will provide the reader with an understanding of the complexity, flexibility, and mental agility required of the troopers in mounted cavalry operations to succeed and return. Truly, this intellectual ability is the mark of a successful cavalryman or any modern warrior. In the course of the Persian Gulf campaign, the 2d Squadron, 4th Cavalry Regiment, added another magnificent chapter in its long and proud heritage.

II. PRELUDE: DEPLOYMENT AND OPERATION DESERT SHIELD

The saga of 2-4 Cav during Operation Desert Storm began long before the lead elements of the squadron crossed the line of departure into Iraq on 24 February 1991. At Fort Stewart, the squadron was known as the 24th Motorized Rifle Battalion. Its primary mission was to conduct opposing forces operations to prepare the Victory Division's armored and mechanized task forces for their National Training Center (NTC) rotations. The squadron had not conducted a squadron-level external training evaluation since its conversion to the J-series table of organization and equipment (TOE) in 1987. In fact, the last squadron-level external evaluation undergone by the unit was as the 2-9 Cav in 1986. The squadron's only NTC rotation occurred in 1985. Additionally, the air cavalry troops had never operated tactically with the ground elements.[3] Thus, the squadron's challenge as it deployed in1990 was evident and daunting.

In spite of these drawbacks, when the war klaxon sounded on 7 August 1990, the 2-4 Cav deployed with the lead brigade of the 24th Infantry Division (Mechanized) (24 ID[M]) as a separate divisional unit that would conduct the full range of cavalry missions in the desert. In fact, the 2-4 Cav was the first U.S. mechanized unit to put teeth into President George Bush's "*line in the sand*" by occupying an 80-kilometer-long screen in the division's security zone along the Tapline Road (approximately 100 kilometers south of the Kuwaiti border).

On 12 July 1990, after having graduated from the U.S. Army Command and General Staff College at Fort Leavenworth, Kansas, I was assigned to the 24th Infantry Division (Mechanized). My primary duty as a member of the G3 section was as the officer in charge of the division's emergency operations center. Less than a month later, at 0100 on 7 August 1990, I handed Major General Barry R. McCaffrey, commanding general of the 24th, the deployment order just received from the XVIII Airborne Corps. The entire message, not more than ten lines long and simply, but profoundly stated, directed the 24 ID(M) to "deploy to CENTCOM [Central Command]." The assistant division commander for support, Colonel Frank Miller, and the chief of staff, Colonel Joe N. Frazar III, were also present in the office as the commanding general decided on the exact wording of the message that would alert the division and soon have a significant impact on every Victory Division soldier and family member. During the conversation, Major General McCaffrey made a comment that I will remember forever. He said, "From this moment on, we will collectively redefine the meaning of 'hard work.'"

The division was alerted at 0300, 7 August 1990. Never in my thirteen years of service had I seen people work harder, longer, or for such high stakes. There was no difference between day and night. Telephone calls at 0200 were answered by civilian secretaries who had been at their desks for twenty hours. Cots were set up in offices and hallways for exhausted souls to catch a few hours of sleep. A field kitchen was set up behind the division headquarters. Scarcely seventy-two hours later, the vehicles began to roll as the division was on the move.

Just six days, nine hours, and fifty-seven minutes following the alert, the FSS Capella, the first of ten ships, began her journey with much of the 2d Brigade's combat team and the 2d Squadron, 4th Cavalry, on board. One of the many duties I performed was to move the division main command post (CP) onto the ship at the port of Savannah. Since I had never seen a division main CP, it was truly an adventure.

On 22 August 1990, I was in charge of moving the division main CP's personnel. We said good-bye to our families, drew our weapons, and spent the next thirty-six hours in a hangar at Hunter Army Airfield awaiting our flight to the Kingdom of Saudi Arabia.

From the outset, Major General McCaffrey envisioned using the 2-4 Cav as a separate unit under his control. In fact, one of the first divisional fragmentary orders (FRAGOs) detached the squadron from the aviation brigade and placed it under divisional control. The detachment highlights one of the fundamental issues surrounding divisional cavalry operations. When the squadron was re-designated the 2d Squadron, 4th Cavalry, in January 1987, it began the process of converting to a new organizational design and equipment. This new divisional cavalry squadron was assigned to the aviation brigade and consisted of two ground cavalry troops and two air cavalry troops.

Each ground troop's combat power consisted primarily of nineteen

In August 1991, Victory Division soldiers rested in a **hangar at Hunter Army Airfield**, Savannah, Georgia, awaiting flights to Saudi Arabia. Even the intense humidity and heat in Georgia paled compared to what they experienced in the port of Ad Dammam.

M3 cavalry fighting vehicles and three M106 mortars. Each air troop had six observation helicopters (OH-58Cs) and four attack helicopters with TOW (tube-launched, optically tracked, wire-guided) capability (AH-1Fs).

The 2-4 Cav's predecessor, the 2-9 Cav, was a much more robust organization in terms of combat power. Each ground troop had twelve main battle tanks and sixteen M113 variants used as scout vehicles, while all the aviation assets were in one air troop under the command of a major. The change in organization and equipment reflected not only a great change in the capabilities but an entirely new command and control arrangement. In essence, the relative lack of combat power created a situation where the squadron could no longer perform many of the combat tasks it previously executed routinely.[4]

The creators of the new austere organization envisioned that the cavalry squadron would perform reconnaissance and screening operations rather than operate as the division's tenth maneuver task force, as was traditional. Certainly, Major General McCaffrey preferred the tenth maneuver task force option, since it would give him the flexibility to deploy a powerful combat unit directly under his control.

On deployment into the desert, TF 2-4 Cav was tailored to perform specific missions under the control of the division commander. First, D Troop, 4th Cavalry (D/4 Cav)--the separate cavalry troop assigned to the 197th Separate Infantry Brigade (197 SIB) from Fort Benning, Georgia--was attached to the squadron when the 197 SIB was deployed as the third maneuver brigade of the 24 ID(M). Of particular note is that the D/4 Cav was organized as a regimental cavalry troop with four platoons. Its two tank platoons consisted of M60A3 tanks and two scout platoons, each with three M113s and three M901 improved TOW vehicles (ITVs), along with a three-tube M106 mortar section.

Second, the division's MLRS (multiple-launch rocket system) battery, A Battery, 13th Field Artillery (A/13 FA), was attached to the task force to provide indirect fire support during the initial screening mission. The battery consisted of nine MLRS launchers. Third, several mechanized infantry and armored teams were attached as they arrived in country, thus increasing the squadron's combat power during the initial occupation of the division's sector.

The first weeks of Operation Desert Shield were indeed uncertain times, as Saddam Hussein's opportunity to attack into Saudi Arabia was a real possibility. Since TF 2-4 Cav was the most forward-deployed U.S. mechanized force, the significant increase in its combat power was warranted and welcome. However, with the integration of these forces, the squadron's leadership was severely taxed, for the unit had not had many opportunities to train as a cavalry squadron, much less as a large task force. Fortunately, this training was fruitful, because a scant five months later, the squadron fought well as a large task force.

Our airplane arrived in the Kingdom of Saudi Arabia's Dahran International Airport at 0600, 23 August 1990. As we deplaned, the flight attendants were in tears and gave us anything we wanted. (I still take my United Airlines blanket with me to the field.) As we exited the plane at about 0630, it was 93 degrees (on the way to 130 that day). At about 1300, we boarded buses to take us to the port of Ad Dammam. It was the longest bus ride of my life, because in true Army fashion every seat on all ten or so buses had to be occupied before the drivers would leave. The result was that the loading process alone took over an hour in the hottest part of the day.

Immediately on arriving at the division forward command post (Victory Forward), I assumed duties as a watch officer in the G3 section. Professionally, I was unprepared for the duty of watch officer under these austere and stressful conditions. But the mission was clear: know everything that was happening in the division. You couldn't fake it. The task, however, was even more difficult than usual because none of the normal communications systems were operational. Clearly, the most frazzled staff officer was the assistant division signal officer, Major Fred Lehman, who passed out while conducting his part of an early nightly update. Planes kept arriving, and ships began to arrive and unload.

One of my primary duties was to be the G3 briefer at the nightly division updates to the commanding general. But with so much happening, these briefings were very difficult, and I was never very sure of anything, and it showed. The first unit to assemble and move out to the desert was TF 2-4 Cav. We tracked the movements of the squadron closely during those early days, even though communications was spotty. Eventually, the task force moved 200 kilometers out in the desert. Everyone was happy to join the squadron in the desert because living in the port was unbearable. But even though the desert was harsh, it lacked the humidity and miserable sanitary conditions found in port.

One day, we discovered that the port area was rife with ammunition-in fact, the ship just outside the division head-quarters was loaded with ammunition-which made the desert appear even more enticing. During my tenure at the G3 section, I was responsible to the commanding general and the G3, Lieutenant Colonel Pat Lamar, for tracking and controlling the operations of the entire division. Specifically, the operations section was charged with monitoring the daily functions of the division's main CP, controlling the liaison officers attached to the main CP, writing and publishing all the division FRAGOs, briefing the command group nightly at the 2000 update, and drafting the commander's daily situation reports that were sent to corps.

Consequently, performing these duties kept me informed of all the activities in the division. Also, the operations section tracked the other U.S. and coalition forces' situations and performed as the division's land management section as more and more units arrived in the theater. From this vantage point, I was able to track the activities of the 2-4 Cav on a daily basis.

The 2-4 Cav now moved to another "frontier," this time along the Tapline Road in Saudi Arabia. The squadron's mission was to execute a screen across the entire division's sector as the division's main body occupied its tactical assembly areas. The squadron was the most forward-deployed U.S. unit until the 3d Armored Cavalry Regiment relieved it on 6 October 1990. This would not be the last time the squadron protected the division's move to occupy tactical assembly areas during the Southwest Asian campaign.

When relieved from the screening mission, the squadron occupied a base camp known as Fort Apache. Here, the squadron was again returned to its organic configuration-with the exception of D/4 Cav, which remained with the squadron for the remainder of the deployment. Immediately, the squadron began its in-country training program.

Training was focused at the platoon and section level because of the training versus readiness dilemma. The very act of maneuver training causes a reduction in readiness because vehicles break down and resources are consumed. Squadron–or troop–size mechanized maneuvers were not conducted because the logistical system during most of Operation Desert Shield could not support the cost of maintaining vehicle readiness due to the extensive track vehicle movement. However, platoon and section standardized training exercises were developed and executed on a regular basis. The requirement for constant readiness forced commanders at all levels constantly to balance the costs of maneuver training with their combat readiness.

Even though the training was at the platoon and section level, individual training never stopped. The squadron built two mounted land navigation courses, a dismounted land navigation course, and a small-arms range. All the M3A1 crews conducted a modified Bradley

Left to right are Sergeant Gary Castille, Specialist Marty Keys, and Private First Class Jay Nolet. **Mail call** was very important. It brought the Stars and Stripes newspaper. The newspapers may not have been very current, but they were always welcome. Contact with the outside world was limited to mail, newspapers, and the radio. Radio reception was spotty and inconsistent. Voice of America was the most reliable.

By far the most important communications were the telephone calls home. AT&T and the division staff did a great job in setting up and operating the phone centers. There were three in the division sector during Operation Desert Shield and AT&T provided a mobile center that moved with the division to the attack positions. A soldier could reasonably expect to make a telephone call home about once a month. The last opportunity the task force had to call was about three days before the start of the ground war.

Gunnery Table VII. In addition, the squadron S2 instituted an aggressive intelligence-training program that he and his staff conducted weekly for the entire squadron at each troop area.

The squadron participated in various force modernization programs that occurred throughout the division. The D/4 Cav fielded both the M1A1, to replace its M60A3s, and added MK-19 automatic grenade launchers to its M113 scout vehicles.[5]

III. TRANSITION TO WAR

As the division's command estimate process had developed and produced the operations plan for Operation Desert Storm, the requirement for a significantly more combat-capable squadron had become evident. Consequently, a division FRAGO was published on or about 20 December 1990, creating TF 2-4 Cav. The task organization of the squadron provided the squadron with the assets for the following missions:

- Conduct 24-hour, all-weather reconnaissance operations.
- Conduct independent security operations with organic combat power.
- Operate in advance of the main body yet under continuous and responsive indirect fire support.
- Sustain operations with the capability to "plug in and out" of any brigade support area or the division support area.
- Command and control rapidly changing task organizations while conducting the full range of cavalry missions.

The resulting task organization is shown in Table 1.

Significant to this new task organization was the loss of the squadron's two air cavalry troops and the aviation unit maintenance troop or E Troop. To enhance logistical support, the division commander consolidated all the aviation assets under the aviation brigade. Also, as was common throughout Operation Desert Storm, the division commander used the air troops to provide the maneuver brigades (and himself) with a rapid reaction force and responsive reconnaissance assets. As discussed earlier, it is clear that the 24 ID(M) utilized the cavalry squadron as an independent maneuver task force.

For many years prior to the implementation of the new organization, the heavy divisions in Germany had detached the air troops to the combat aviation battalions, leaving the squadron proper to operate as a totally ground maneuver force. In fact, these squadrons boasted thirty-six tanks, eighteen TOW missile tracks, and eighteen scout M113s with Dragon antitank missile launchers.

These European squadrons had more organic combat power than

the tank or mechanized infantry battalions. Again, these squadrons were used as the tenth maneuver battalion that performed cavalry missions.

TABLE 1

TF 2-4 Cav's Task Organization for Reconnaissance and Security Operations

TF 2-4 CAV

A/2-4 CAV (19 M3A1; 3 M106)
1-2/3/GSR/B/124 MI (DS)
SEC/7/25 CHEM (RECON-F) (DS)
1/A/3 ENG (CBT) (DS)

D/4 CAV (9 M1A1; 6 M901; 6 M113; 3 M106)
3-4/3/GSR/B/124 MI (DS)
SEC/7/25 CHEM (RECON-F) (DS)
3/A/3 ENG (CBT) (DS)

D/3-69 AR (14 M1A1)
2/A/3 ENG (CBT) (DS)

A/13 FA (MLRS) (9 LAUNCHERS)
Q37/G/333 FA (TAB) (DS)
1-4/ADA/HHC/197 BDE (STINGER) (DS)

A/3 ENG(-) (CBT) (DS)

1-3/1/4/B/1-5 ADA (STINGER) (DS)

1-4/2/4/B/1-5 ADA (STINGER) (DS)

5/91 CHEM (SMOKE) (DS)

C/124 MI (DS)
1/2/C/519/525/XVII ABN CORPS (EW) (DS)
1/3/C/519/525/XVII ABN CORPS (EW) (DS)

3/1/B/124 MI (IPW) (DS)

TACP (DS)

SQUADRON TRAINS
LOGISTICS SUPPORT TEAM(LST) 724 SB (MAIN)
MAINT TEAM 224 SB (FWD)
MAINT TEAM 197 SB (FWD)

(The total number of troopers ranged from 1,250 to 1,375 with approximately 250 vehicles.)

On 18 January 1991, the air cavalry troops were detached from TF 2-4 Cav and attached to the aviation brigade as TF Air Cav. Commander of TF Air Cav was the former executive officer of the squadron, Major L. Clay Edwards. This attachment continued throughout the war, with the air cavalry troops being assigned to the operational control (OPCON) of many different units for brief periods to accomplish specific missions.

As the new task force began to assemble at Fort Apache, the squadron commander realized that this change in task organization created an immediate training challenge. Therefore, the squadron began conducting various command and control exercises known as TOCEXs (tactical operations center exercises). These internal exercises significantly improved the squadron's command and control systems.

Christmas at Fort Apache. The small white Haj tent was the chapel. Note the Christmas tree held up by reindeer. Tires, like those in the foreground, marked the roads in the desert. Often the roads and helipads in and around encampments were doused with fuel in order to control the dust created by vehicle traffic on the powdery sand surfaces.

Also, in December 1990, the squadron commander instituted a vigorous leader training program to familiarize all the elements of the task force with cavalry operations. This warfighter exercise began with classes on the capabilities of all the elements of the task force. Then, the squadron leaders, down to and including platoon sergeants, conducted walk-through rehearsals, graduating to HMMWV (high-mobility multipurpose wheeled vehicle) mounted field training exercises. Finally, the squadron conducted a two-day mounted field-training exercise with the leaders mounted in their combat vehicles. This week-long training event significantly increased the squadron's level of confidence in its ability to perform established standard tactics, techniques, and procedures.[6]

A mobile post exchange (PX). Units were required to provide their own personnel to operate the PX. Each unit was required to open an account with the PX and operate it with a detailed soldier. Because of the wide separation of the troops, the PX remained mobile in one of the locally procured vehicles. The cross-country mobility required in the desert was not friendly to these vehicles. Note the door strapped to the top of the vehicle and the cardboard replacement on the driver's side.

IV. ORGANIZATION FOR COMBAT

The unusual task organization of TF 2-4 Cav required modification to the tactics, techniques, and procedures prescribed in FM 17-95, Cavalry Operations. The squadron was organized with a forward tactical command post (TAC CP), a main command post or tactical operations center (TOC), and an administrative and logistics operations center (ALOC), which served as the rear command post. The ALOC controlled both the combat trains that were collated with it and the field trains that normally were located with the brigade support area (BSA) closest to the squadron's area of operations.

The TAC CP consisted of two M3Als and one M113A2 that belonged to the air liaison officer. The officer in charge of the TAC CP was the operations officer (S3). The squadron commander (SCO) fought from the TAC CP and returned to the TOC as required. He rode with the air liaison officer in the M113A2 assigned to the TAC CP. This vehicle with its multiple radios, to include ultra high frequency (UHF) and very high frequency (VHF) radios (which could communicate with all types of aircraft), gave the SCO the most efficient mobile communications capability possible. Also, the SCO preferred the M113A2 to the M3A1 as a command and control vehicle primarily because of the size of the crew compartment. The S3 operated from an M3A1, with the other M3A1 serving primarily as a security vehicle for the other two vehicles. The TAC CP was positioned forward and was usually found moving with the lead troop.

The TOC consisted of five M577s (command post vehicles) and various wheeled vehicles. The five M577s were for the S2, S3, fire support officer, engineer, and communications (RATT [radio and teletype] Rig). The officer in charge of the TOC was the squadron executive officer (SXO), and the non-commissioned officer (NCO) in charge was the operations sergeant major. The staff officers who worked in the TOC were the S2, two battle captains from the operations section, the fire support officer, the flight operations officer, the engineer company executive officer, and the signal officer.

All of the officers and soldiers of the TOC worked directly for the SXO and sergeant major. The TOC was responsible for controlling the current operations, planning for future operations, issuing plans and orders, coordinating service support, and coordinating with all

Command group M113A2. This M113A2 armored personnel carrier was authorized for the air liaison officer's section. The task force commander fought from this vehicle because of the added radios and the crew compartment gave him the space to command the task force. The vehicle had a UHF radio for communicating with aircraft and a more reliable global positioning system.

The commander's cavalry fighting vehicle, commanded by Staff Sergeant James Gill, provided security for the command M113 and the operations officer's cavalry fighting vehicle. Staff Sergeant Gill had the keenest ability to navigate in the desert without any navigational aids. His vehicle broke down the night before the task force crossed into Iraq. By himself, Gill navigated over 200 kilometers to rejoin the task force. These three vehicles made up the command group.

higher and flank elements. Because of the distances involved, the SCO rarely could communicate with the squadron's higher headquarters during the conduct of combat operations. Consequently, the tactical satellite (TACSAT) radio located at the TOC provided the most reliable link to the division and brigades. The SXO regularly used the TACSAT radio, which was not mobile, to transmit and receive messages and orders. When in range, the FM (frequency modulation) radio was also used for communications, and when the TOC was moving, it became the only means of communications.

The TOC moved independently under the control of the SXO to ensure the availability of constant communications with subordinate and higher units. Therefore, the TOC's position was generally in the center of the sector of operations but was not collated with any combat forces. Thus, the TOC was responsible for its own security.

The combat trains consisted of the ALOC, support platoon, and a small S1/S4 section. The maintenance soldiers manned the unit maintenance collection point (UMCP) and most of the squadron maintenance platoon under the control of the squadron maintenance officer. The S4 was in charge of the combat trains, and their mission was consistent with prescribed doctrine, except that the entire combat service support (CSS) organization of the cavalry squadron reflected the multifaceted face of the task force.

Included in the combat trains were a logistical support team from the 724th Main Support Battalion and maintenance support teams from the 197th and 224th Forward Support Battalions. The first sergeants controlled the logistical assets for the troops and were located forward with the troop combat trains.[7]

When this large task force was formed, the division's commanding general recognized that a deputy commander (DCO) was needed to assist the task force commander. As a result, on Christmas Day of 1990, Major Louis Gelling Jr., a former executive officer of the 3-69 Armor, became the new DCO. During combat operations, the DCO was responsible primarily for the task force's logistical support, and he operated primarily from the ALOC. If required, he would move to the TOC and then to the TAC CP to assume command of the task force. In the interim, the executive officer would assume command until the deputy could move forward.[8]

The squadron maintenance officer was responsible for the UMCP. He established UMCPs, reported their location, managed the maintenance assets available, and moved them in order to maintain rapid and responsive maintenance support for the forward elements. The standard for the establishment of an UMCP was to tow damaged vehicles with internal recovery assets until all the recovery assets were towing a piece of equipment. When the next vehicle broke down, all the towed vehicles would be dropped and an UMCP established under the control of the senior maintenance officer or NCO on site.

TF 2-4 Cav's main command post TOC during the reconnaissance and security phase. From left to right are the engineer, fire support, operations, and intelligence M577 command post vehicles. Note the TACSAT radio antenna next to the far right M577. The antenna requires "aiming" at the satellite for operations. The radio was not mobile. The task force had one of only five in the division. Note the MSQ-103 electronic intelligence interceptor assigned to C Company, 124th Military Intelligence Battalion, during the reconnaissance and security phase.

NOTE: The main command post had three configurations: SUPER HOT, HOT, and COLD. SUPER HOT was a short halt to establish communications since the TACSAT radio was not mobile. HOT was for longer stops and used predominantly throughout the war. COLD was for stationary operations over the longer term. The configuration shown is the COLD TOC.

All the recovery assets would then continue forward and catch up with the main body, picking up more damaged vehicles. As vehicles at the UMCP became operational, the entire group would move forward to be either returned to the unit or consolidated with another UMCP. During Operation Desert Storm, five UMCPs were established. This system proved very responsive in returning repaired equipment to the troops as soon as possible.

The headquarters and headquarters troop (HHT) commander was the officer in charge of the field trains and was collated during most of Operation Desert Storm with the 224th Forward Support Battalion, which was in direct support of the 2d Brigade. His primary responsi-

TF 2-4 Cav's main command post in a configuration that featured one extension to facilitate night operations and to protect the crew from the elements. Notice the two-tone camouflage pattern on the vehicles. This pattern was used on all cavalry vehicles prior to deployment because it identified the vehicle as belonging to the opposing forces while the squadron was at Fort Stewart. Also notice the right side up "V," which was displayed on all Victory Division vehicles. The inverted "V" was an identification symbol on all coalition vehicles.

bility was to push resupply assets forward after they had returned to the BSA. In essence, he coordinated the movement of CSS assets between the combat trains and the various supply points within the BSA or division support area (DSA). The HHT commander would then organize and provide command and control for the resupply convoys as they moved back to the combat trains. The field trains were authorized to receive support from any BSA or the DSA, depending on their proximity to the squadron's area of operations.[9]

V. TF 2-4 CAV AT WAR

The wartime saga of TF 2-4 Cav began on 16 January 1991. On that day, at 0300, the task force TOC received the message from the CENTCOM commander in chief, General H. Norman Schwarzkopf, declaring the beginning of the war. As planes screamed overhead on the first air attack into Iraq, the troopers of TF 2-4 Cav sat in marshaling area Victory just north of Jelady, Saudi Arabia, waiting for heavy equipment transporters (HETs) and tractor-trailers to transport them into position approximately 50 kilometers due south of Nisab, Saudi Arabia, a distance of over 500 kilometers.

On 22 January 1991, while waiting for transportation to the pre-attack positions, the squadron commander was medically evacuated and Major Gelling assumed command of the task force.

Major Louis Gelling Jr. assumed command of the task force during the occupation of the security zone in the vicinity of Nisab, Saudi Arabia.

At 0330, 23 January, the task force began loading onto HETs in preparation for the 500-kilometer move northwest along the Tapline Road. At 2000, 24 January, the task force moved out to occupy a security zone along the Saudi Arabian-Iraqi border. The task force moved in seventeen serials to its new assembly area on 25 January

1991. Tapline Road is basically a service road fifteen to twenty feet wide that had been used to service the Arabian-American Oil Company pipeline. During the campaign, this service road was used to support most of the coalition force. Since this road was extremely busy, accidents were a regular occurrence. All the crews of the tracked vehicles were aboard their vehicles, carried on HETs.

Hinesville In order to ensure that members of the division did not miss the turnoff at the Tapline Road, this sign was erected. The long road march along the Tapline Road into the attack positions seemed to last forever. Hinesville, Georgia, is the home of the 24th Infantry Division (Mechanized). By this time, every trooper knew that the road to Hinesville went right through Iraq.

Since local nationals drove the HETs, convoy control was challenging, and rarely did a convoy arrive in the same configuration as it began. Further aggravating the situation was the weather, which was rainy and cold. For operational security reasons, movement was conducted mostly at night. Upon arrival, the task force moved out immediately to occupy positions along the Saudi Arabian-Iraqi border.

The security zone was seventy kilometers wide and ten kilometers deep. The task force's missions were as follows:

- Clear the zone of any enemy forces.
- Guard the main body of the division as it occupied assembly areas and eventually attack positions.
- Conduct a zone reconnaissance of the security zone, which would assist in the planning of the attack by identifying all physical structures along the border and also in analyzing specific terrain features that included the berm that ran along the border.
- Conceal, through limited daylight operations, the buildup of the division.

Specifically, protecting the force was the critical task that the commanding general had assigned the task force.[10]

Upon arrival in the forward assembly area, the task force quickly deployed into the sector, clearing the security zone (see Map 1). The security zone was initially established as a ten-kilometer-deep zone along the Saudi Arabian-Iraqi border. Later, the security zone was increased to include a ten-kilometer zone on the Iraqi side of the border, as the need for cross-border combat information became necessary. No enemy forces were discovered, and the task force occupied the sector without incident.

On 29 January 1991, Lieutenant Colonel Thomas J. Leney assumed command of TF 2-4 Cav. Leney had been slated to take command of the squadron in the spring of 1991, but because he was needed to assume command of TF 2-4 Cav immediately, the chief of staff of the Army directed him on 24 January to depart Washington for Southwest Asia.

Between 29 January and 3 February, the squadron staff was reorganized. Major Joseph C. Barto III came from the division G3 section to assume duties as the squadron executive officer, and Captain Peter Utley, the assistant S3, became the operations officer (S3). Captain Karl Buchanan arrived from the division G2 section to assume duties as the intelligence officer (S2). Captain Rans Black, a battle captain in the division tactical command post, assumed duties as a battle captain, and Captain Jeffrey Bierl, who had come directly from the Armor Officer Advanced Course, assumed duties as the other battle captain.

The last significant change in the battle staff occurred on 20 February 1991 when Master Sergeant (P) Bernard Cabrerra, a 2-4 Cav veteran, arrived after a long and arduous journey to assume duties as the operations sergeant major. All of these staff changes occurred while the squadron performed security operations for the division. For the new commander and these new staff officers, it was truly a baptism under fire, and they responded in true cavalry fashion - Prepared and Loyal.

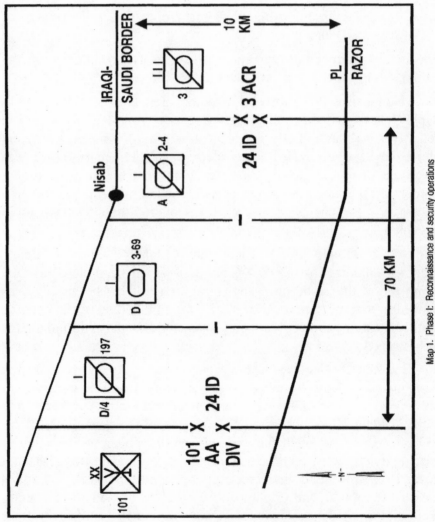

Map 1. Phase I: Reconnaissance and security operations

I quickly dressed, wondering what had gone wrong now. When I arrived at the main command post, the G3 shook my hand and everyone was looking at me as if they knew something that I didn't. Just then, Major General McCaffrey came out of his van and took me back to his sleeping van, which was located with the main CP. My mind was racing and I had no idea what was next. He put his hand on my shoulder and said, "I'm putting you in; tomorrow you will be the executive officer of the Cav." Holy Jesus! I was totally taken aback. My mind raced. This seasoned warrior sensed my astonishment. It was like getting hit in the chest with a baseball bat.

By this time, I knew we would fight, but we didn't know when. I thought of my family and knew I would not be able to tell my wife because no telephones were available. Going from the relative safety of the main CP down to the Cav and being the unit first into Iraq was quite a change for one of the most junior majors in the division.

My second thought was for the soldiers I would lead. Was I good enough for them? I knew the Cav because I had commanded a cavalry troop in the 3d Armored Division in Germany, but that was five years ago. McCaffrey took some time to express his confidence in me and since there was a brand new squadron commander, he wanted someone who knew the division and its leadership to take the job.

Also, he told me that I was to run the task force's TOC. I told him I would not let him down and I immediately returned to my tent to write my wife and to pack my bags. I could not begin to recount all the thoughts that went through my mind for the next twenty-four hours, but I knew that starting the next day, I would have soldiers depending on me to do the right thing. I spent most of those few hours praying for the strength and fortitude to carry the day. That night, at my last 2000 update at the main CP, I told the assembled group with whom I had experienced so much, that I had spent most of my adult life preparing myself to lead men in combat. Now, it was time for me to summon all of my professional and personal courage and competence and perform.

The next morning (2 February) at 0630, Major Greg Stone arrived at my tent and I took off for the Cav. It was my wife's birthday. When I arrived at the task force TOC, a command and staff meeting was in progress. As I gazed across the room, I did not see many

TF 2-4 Cav's assumption of command ceremony along the Iraqi-Saudi Arabian border. The division commander, Major General Barry R. McCaffrey, presided and Major (P) Louis Gelling Jr. was the commander of troops.

friendly faces. To them, I was another change in the leadership of the squadron that had been constantly changing over the previous month or so.

After the war, several of the junior officers told me that this was a very strange time for them. The joke among them was that you had better not go to the TOC because you might never come back. For five officers, to include the squadron commander, three staff officers, and one platoon leader, this was true. I had never met the new squadron commander and he had been in command for exactly four days. Fortunately, I had known many of the new officers from my time at division. The DCO, Major Lou Gelling, and I had known each other from his days as the deputy G1 at the division main CP. The new S2, Captain Karl "Buck" Buchanan, and Captain Rans Black were also familiar from my time at the division main. Also, because of my duties in the G3 operations section, I had had regular contact with many of the members of the task force TOC over the radio and telephone for the past six months.

I attribute my initial acceptance by these seasoned desert troopers to several factors. First, Major Greg Stone spent the first day introducing me to the staff and explaining the current situation and operations procedures. Second, Major Gelling's astute assessments of the command environment in the task force quickly

-26-

brought to light the challenge I faced. Third, from my previous duties, I had an accurate view of the "big picture." This perspective was much appreciated by everyone.

Immediately following the command and staff meeting, the SCO met with the command group and clearly defined roles, responsibilities, and the chain of command. Major Gelling was second in command and responsible for the logistical operations of the task force. The S1, S4, squadron maintenance officer, medical platoon leader, surgeon, and chaplain worked directly for him. I was in charge of the TOC, and the S2, fire support officer, air liaison officer, flight operations officer, and battle captains worked directly for me. Specifically, I was charged with control of the current operations and the planning for future operations. Therefore, for planning, the S3 also operated under my purview.

The next morning, 3 February, I drove Major Stone back to the division main command post where he assumed my previous duties in the G3 section. On the way back to the task force, I collected two new officer replacements: Captain Jeff Bierl and Second Lieutenant Wayne White. Both had just arrived in country, and Jeff was to be the other battle captain in the TOC, while Wayne would be the medical platoon leader. Already, I was not the newest officer in the squadron.

Because of a blinding sandstorm, the drive back to the TOC, which normally took one hour, took over three hours. This was my first experience with the difficulty in navigating in zero-visibility conditions using only a compass and odometer. This was not very accurate. Many of my first excursions in the desert were successful only because I stopped at units along the way and asked them for their grid locations. I then used that data to plot a new azimuth and direction and off we would go.

With every passing minute, my confidence grew. I knew from my previous experience at division how to run the current operations of a TOC. My recent training at the Command and General Staff College gave me confidence in my ability to plan operations using the command estimate process. These, combined with my knowledge of the "big picture," set the stage for me to step right in and contribute. First, though, I had to communicate my expectations to the soldiers in the TOC.

That afternoon, I gathered all the troopers in the TOC and began to establish my standard of operations in the TOC. First, I explained that the role of the TOC is to control the operations of the task force. Control is based on the TOC's capacity to gather accurate and pertinent information so the commander can make informed decisions. Therefore,the TOC must always be in communication with all the subordinate units, friendly forces around the task force, and higher headquarters.

An efficient TOC must be able to collate a lot of information into a clear picture of the battlefield and communicate that picture to the commander for decisions. Then, once a decision is made, he must coordinate, develop, and execute a plan that brings all the battlefield operating systems to bear at the critical place and time on the battlefield. Finally, using all of this information, we had to anticipate future situations and prepare for them. Our challenge was to paint the most accurate picture of the battlefield as possible. Accuracy in the TOC means the reduction of "TOC time" to real time.

After receiving input from the TOC personnel, I immediately established two twelve-hour shifts and assigned a battle captain and an operations NCO in charge of each shift. I stressed that everyone in the TOC is an information gatherer, but that information only becomes useful when it gets to the battle captain who is standing in front of an updated map continually assessing the situation and updating the commander. The S2, fire support officer, flight operations officer, S3 sergeant major, and I were not scheduled for any shift but were constantly available for action. Also, this group, along with the S3, was the essence of the planning group.

The TOC's responsibility is to monitor both current operations- the battle captain's primary duty-and concurrently plan future operations. With this reorganization, a quick training class, and a pep talk, the TOC personnel went back to work. Even though we were in the midst of combat, the TOC crew underwent training events every day. Some training was "hip pocket," like chemical training or proper techniques in updating map boards or correctly receiving spot reports. Some training was larger in scope. For example, one day, we passed control of the task force to the TAC and trained the TOC on movement techniques and various TOC configurations. Training

The winter of 1991 was one of the wettest for Saudi Arabia. This bunker filled with water shows how miserable living conditions could become when it rained in the desert. The hard-surface roads were mostly petroleum based, which became slicker than ice when it rained. The Tapline Road was one such surface.

must continue in combat because it is the only way to correct shortcomings in operational procedures.

On my arrival at the task force TOC, I was shocked by the austere living conditions. Not all the troopers had a covered place to sleep. The weather was cold for the area, and soldiers slept on the ground or in their vehicles. All the cots were left at Fort Apache, but most of the troopers had acquired Saudi-made foam rolls to serve as mattresses. The usually brightly colored mats were the only thing between the troops and the ground in most cases.

In preparation for combat, the task force had "lightened up" before leaving Fort Apache. For example, all my driver had was his rucksack loaded with one desert-camouflage uniform, three changes of underwear and socks, personal hygiene items, and his sleeping bag. All the task force troopers, and for that matter the entire division, were wearing chemical protective over-garments.

Haircut day in the desert. With a sharp set of clippers a "good" barber could give twenty haircuts an hour.

The division had gone to mission-oriented protection posture (MOPP) level I at the outbreak of hostilities on 16 January and remained in the chemical protective suits until the war was over and we were back in Saudi Arabia-a period of over eight weeks. These suits were not conducive to good personal hygiene, for a clean hand pushed through the charcoal-lined sleeve would emerge black. In spite of this, the entire chain of command constantly stressed personal hygiene and ensured that it was conducted daily. The task force TOC was provided logistical resupply daily, which normally consisted of food, fuel, mail, any general supplies, and water. The food was meals, ready-to-eat (MREs), with one hot meal provided every two days. Packages from home provided much appreciated supplements to the MREs.

A field-expedient shower. Personal hygiene was always a challenge in the desert. Laundry was an especially difficult problem because of the logistics and distance involved. In combat operations, laundry and personal hygiene are important morale issues. The rule in the division was that each soldier would get a pot of hot water every morning for personal hygiene.

VI. RECONNAISSANCE AND SECURITY MISSION

Initially, the division G2 was responsible for the planning and execution of the division's reconnaissance and security (R&S) operations. However, on 3 February 1991, the commanding general assigned total responsibility for the division's R&S operations to TF 2-4 Cav under the direct supervision of Brigadier General James T. Scott, the assistant division commander (maneuver) (ADC[M]). Consequently, from 3 February until it was relieved on 20 February, just days before G-day, the task force controlled all the forces and operations in the security zone. The task force battle staff quickly developed a plan and immediately began its execution.

The overriding mission of the R&S plan was twofold: to protect the force and to detail exactly the physical environment and enemy situation in the border area in order to support future operations.

To allow for maximum coverage of the seventy-by-ten-kilometer zone, extra units were added to the task force. The task force realized quickly that before the offensive began, the entire division's focus was on operations in the security zone. Therefore, any divisional asset was available for use in the security zone. Ultimately, all scout platoons from the maneuver brigades were attached to the task force for varying periods of time. In addition, an air cavalry troop was collocated with the task force TOC for use during daylight operations.

At night, two OH-58Ds were at the TOC with an AH-64 Apache Company on standby. Both the OH-58D and the AH-64 helicopters have a night operations capability not found in the OH-58C and AH-1 helicopters assigned to the air cavalry. Also, the AH-64s, with their precision laser designation capability, provided and confirmed cross-border information.

Six civilian land cruisers were also attached to the task force when troops conducted reconnaissance close to the border. All of these assets were used to identify, and then confirm, the physical terrain features along the border. The task force instituted a policy difficulty in identifying the locations of physical structures. It was a constant struggle to confirm the border trace and all the nuances of the zone.

The S2, Captain Karl Buchanan, briefs at the daily reconnaissance and security briefing. At the left is the task force's planning map. This briefing tent was adjacent to the TOC.

Air Cavalry. During the R&S phase, the task force had one air cavalry troop and two OH-58Ds collated with the task force's main command post. These assets were integrated into the concept of the operation and assigned information-gathering missions in conjunction with the ground troops.

The air troops operated during the day and the OH-58Ds at night. AH-64swere on call. The air assets were always handed off to the ground commander in whose sector they were operating. Often, there was no flying because of the weather conditions.

The SCO returned from the division main command post at about 2400 on 3 February 1991 and immediately summoned me. At the TOC, the SCO informed me that the commanding general had given us the responsibility for the division's R&S mission. He gave me his commander's guidance and informed me that we would brief the ADC(M), Brigadier General Terry Scott, on our plan at 1000 the next day. Since my arrival in the task force two days earlier, I had had about four hours of sleep, and now, the pressure was on.

I called the battle staff together and started to work. During this time, the battle staff and the entire TOC was molded into a high-performance war fighting team. We were forced to produce a plan and begin its execution within twenty-four hours. We worked all night and received the final modifications from the SCO at 0900. The ADC(M) approved our plan with minor modifications and then informed us that we would brief the division commander at 1500 that same day. After a quick breath and an MRE, we briefed the commanding general, who also approved our plan with few modifications.

At 1630, the order was briefed to the task force and we began its execution. The success of the R&S planning effort under such extreme time constraints gave everyone in the TOC confidence, and you could feel the morale of the TOC begin to rise. Now we knew we could perform. The planning group passed the order over to the battle captain for execution, and the planners began to plan the task force's attack into Iraq. My days became somewhat routine. Rest was critical. The SCO or I were always near the TOC, if not in the TOC. To ensure that a complete briefing occurred, I made sure I was present at each shift change at 1200 and 2400. A lot happened in twelve hours and it was critical that the new shift was completely briefed. I also used the shift changes to conduct training and to give any guidance, because during the shift changes, all the personnel assigned were present.

Rest was essential, both physical and mental. I usually got three or four hours of sleep at night and I tried to take a short nap in the afternoon. In addition, I found that spending twenty minutes a day listening to music, writing a letter, or reading a novel significantly improved my intellectual ability to think clearly, assimilate information, communicate succinctly, and make decisions.

The task force's previous leadership had already done a lot of work on the attack plan, but since neither the SCO nor myself had been involved in its development, we started the command estimate process over again. The review of the plan did not require a complete revision because Captain Pete Utley had written most of it as the assistant S3. Now as the S3, he provided the institutional knowledge facilitating our review, however, the plan was constantly being revised at division level, which caused continuous review within the task force.

I believe that those first days established the bond of trust and confidence between the new commander and his even newer executive officer. After those first two successful briefings, the SCO entrusted me and the TOC crew almost entirely with the planning and execution of the R&S mission. He recognized that he had to get out with the troops and assess the level of training and morale in the task force.

Lieutenant Colonel Leney had already been selected to command the squadron, but he was surprised to be sent into the breach with such little notice and under such difficult conditions. He recognized that he had to get out with the troops now and look them in the eye. Therefore, from 5 to 11 February, he spent much of his time moving from platoon to platoon and spending time with the soldiers. Also, he personally observed the platoon leaders' operations orders and rehearsals for their various missions in support of the R&S plan. Often, he stayed to observe the execution of the operations. These trips were very effective, and I could see the confidence of the SCO and the task force increase.

Beginning on 4 February, the daily division R&S meeting was held at 1600 at the TF 2-4 Cav TOC. The ADC(M) chaired the meeting and representatives from the aviation brigade; 1st 2d, and 197th Brigades; Division G2 and G3; and 124th Military Intelligence Battalion attended. The agenda of the meeting is shown in Table 2.

For a successful R&S mission, all activities were to focus on and support one of the priority information requests (PIRs). If a mission did not relate to a PIR, it was generally disapproved by the ADC(M).

All operations in the security zone were executed under the control of TF 2-4 Cav. No unit could enter the ten-kilometer security zone without prior coordination with TF 2-4 Cav and then only in accordance with the approved R&S operations for that particular period.

Table 2. Reconnaissance and Security Meeting Agenda

Subject	Briefer
Summary of last twenty-four hours of operations	S3
Combat information obtained during last twenty-four hours	S2
Review of all information available and update of priority information requests	S2
Review, refinement, and issuance of final operations orders for next twenty-four hours of operations	S3/Units
Recommendations for missions to be conducted during the 24- to 72-hour period	S3
Nominations for intelligence targets during the 24- to 72-hour period	S3/Units
Guidance and approval for future missions	ADC(M)

The OH-58Ds and AH-64s from the aviation brigade were utilized primarily for night operations and an air cavalry troop was used for daylight operations. Needless to say, throughout this period, there was rarely a quiet moment in the TF 2-4 Cav TOC. The task force commander's intent was not to execute more than one mission at a time because coordinating simultaneous operations over the wide frontage was difficult and fratricide was a concern. However, because of the large amount of information that had to be obtained, R&S missions were being constantly executed. Also, the entire border area was continuously and routinely being observed by either mounted or dismounted observation points (Ops).

During the execution of the R&S plan, the squadron coordinated and executed missions in the following order:

- Cleared the security zone of any enemy forces. No enemy contact was made.

- Observed and cataloged all Iraqi movement in the border area.
- Cataloged the physical characteristics of the border.
- Conducted limited combat operations to destroy any Iraqi reconnaissance assets, thus preventing the enemy from gaining any information about the division.
- Guarded against revealing the division's operations by conducting low-profile R&S operations.

During the R&S mission, which was conducted according to established doctrine, TF 2-4 Cav protected the force from Iraqi detection and gained all the combat information required to ensure that the division's initial attack would be successful. During the operation, the task force observed enemy patrols on approximately ten separate occasions; however, the enemy was never taken under direct fire. On 11 February, A Troop conducted the first cross-border operation with a dismounted area reconnaissance and, therefore, has the distinction of being the first unit in the division to cross into Iraq.[11]

On 14 February 1991, the task force assisted a large Bedouin family and its herd of sheep in crossing the frontier. This family had been traveling extensively through Iraq for several weeks and was desperately trying to move across the border into the relative safety of Saudi Arabia. According to this family, between lack of food, hostile Iraqis, and air strikes, the southern portion of Iraq was not a very hospitable place. Local sources had told this family that no Iraqi soldiers were in the vicinity of Nisab, so they attempted to cross in the task force's sector. In fact, Iraqi Army units had turned this family away at other sites to the east.

Family members reported that they had not seen any Iraqi troops for the last several days, which corroborated the increasingly accurate intelligence picture. The only Iraqi units we had observed were irregular border patrols that usually were mounted in light wheeled vehicles.[12] Being a well-trained American unit used to the very predictable Soviet model to build an enemy order of battle, the lack of an enemy presence caused tremendous hand wringing.

As the battle staff planned for the offensive, entire Iraqi order of battle plans were extracted from even the most sketchy, unreliable information. U.S. combat operations planning begins with an enemy situation found in one of the books in the S2 track. Since the Iraqis would not display it, the battle staff created it and wasted a lot of precious time planning for extremely unlikely events.

Because of the sustained nature of the R&S mission, the troopers of the task force could not humanly maintain the constant state of readiness required for successful mission accomplishment. Therefore, the task force established a cavalry stables assembly area where, for twenty-four hours, platoons were replaced by the battalion scout platoons, pulled off the screen line, and afforded an opportunity to rest and reconstitute.

Basically, a platoon would move into the cavalry stables, where the squadron maintenance section performed maintenance work, the vehicles were downloaded and repacked according to load plan, a hot meal was served, a shower point was established, chapel services were conducted, and tents were provided for the weary troopers for a solid night's sleep.

The squadron command Sergeant Major, Jean L. Soucy, personally supervised the execution of the cavalry stables and spoke with virtually every trooper, either individually or collectively, to assess the level of morale-as anxiety levels began to increase as G-day (the day the ground war would begin) approached. This program paid tremendous dividends by increasing the combat readiness of the task force.[13]

On 19 February 1991, Captain "Buck" Buchanan and I conducted our final R&S briefing at the division main command post. Since responsibility for the security zone was going to be transferred to the maneuver brigades the next day, we were summoned to brief the commanding general and all the brigade commanders. The briefing summarized all the activities in the security zone since 3 February. This changeover briefing went very well and I had flashbacks of all the briefings I had given the general from my days in G3. The commanding general was very pleased with the task force's performance throughout the conduct of this complicated and difficult mission.

At the conclusion of the briefing, we were very proud of our accomplishments. We celebrated our success with all the members of the TOC with sodas and candy we had liberated from the mess hall at the division main command post. The next day, we focused on preparing for the attack into Iraq.

Cavalry stables assembly area

The stables area where the cavalrymen took care of their "mounts"

The shower point was the most popular station at the cavalry stables. The water was cold but plentiful, supplied by the 5,000-gallon water tanker shown on the right.

Command Sergeant Major Jean L. Soucy (at right) was responsible for the cavalry stables .Division Command Sergeant Major James D. Randolph visited this day.

Command Sergeant Major Soucy's area was a natural attraction for all troopers while in the cavalry stables. He always had a warm cup of coffee, encouragement, and counsel. Being one of the few combat veterans of the task force, he was sought out for advice by officers and troopers alike.

VII. PREPARATION FOR THE ATTACK

On 20 February 1991, TF 2-4 Cav was relieved of the reconnaissance and security mission and ordered to pull back to Tactical Assembly Area (TAA) Quarter and prepare for offensive combat operations. The three maneuver brigades moved forward and assumed control of the portion of the security zone in their sectors.

Upon relief from the security mission, TF 2-4 Cav was attached to the 2d Brigade. C Company, 124th Military Intelligence Battalion (C/124 MI) was detached from the task force and attached directly to the 2d Brigade. D/4 Cav was further detached and attached to the 197th Brigade for the initial attack. D/4 Cav would return to the task force's control after Phase Line (PL) Lion was secured. To support D/4Cav, the task force formed "light trains" that were D/4 Cav's normal logistical support elements, which were sent to the 197th Brigade with the D/4 Cav under the control of adjutant, Captain Dave Andersen. The resulting task organization is shown in Table 3.

During a four-day period, the task force conducted rehearsals, issued the final operations order, attended the 2d Brigade's rehearsal, received a briefing and pep talk by the commanding general, and opened and operated test-fire ranges for all crew-served and personal weapons. Also, many troopers phoned home one last time. The rehearsals were extremely important and contributed immeasurably to the squadron's success during the battle. Since the formation of the task force in early January, no task force-level maneuver had occurred. To remedy this situation, for two intense days, during the day and at night, the task force rehearsed movement techniques and drills. These rehearsals gave everyone in the task force confidence in its ability to maneuver, fight, and accomplish the mission.

Additionally, the task force participated in a night tactical exercise without troops (TEWT) with the 2d Brigade, which gave the leaders confidence in the plan. Following the final rehearsal, each troop moved to individual assembly areas and completed preparations for combat operations, to include the opening of test-fire ranges for weapons up to the 25-mm guns on the M3Als.

No tank main-gun test firing was authorized. Finally, on 21 February, the commanding general visited the task force leaders and reviewed the plan. The squadron commander back-briefed the commanding general on the task force's plan, and the commanding general concluded the session with an inspirational talk that left all in attendance with an understanding of the "big picture" and the assurance that we had the complete trust and confidence of the division commander. All the leaders present felt the quiet confidence that we were prepared for the task ahead. That night,the task force leaders assembled at the TOC and conducted their final map exercise (MAPEX) and back-brief.

Table 3. TF 2-4 Cav's Task Organization for Combat Operations

TF 2-4 CAV
    A/2-4 CAV (19 M3A1; 3 M106)
        1-2/3/GSR/B/124 MI (DS)
        1/A/3 ENG (CBT) (DS)
    D/3-69 AR (14 M1A1)

    A/13 FA (MLRS) (9 LAUNCHERS)
        Q37/G/333 FA (TAB) (DS)
        1-4/ADA/HHC/197 BDE (STINGER) (DS)
        2/A/3 ENG (CBT) (DS)
    A/3 ENG(-) (CBT) (DS)
        1-3/1/4/B/1-5 ADA (STINGER) (DS)
        1-4/2/4/B/1-5 ADA (STINGER) (DS)
    SEC/7/25 CHEM (RECON-F) (DS)
    TACP (DS)

    SQUADRON TRAINS (-)
        LOGISTICS SUPPORT TEAM(LST) 724 SB (MAIN)
        MAINT TEAM 224 SB (FWD)
        MAINT TEAM 197 SB (FWD)

NOTE: D/4 Cav was detached from the task force and attached to 197th Brigade. It returned to task force control upon arrival on PL Lion.

    D/4 CAV (9 M1A1; 6 M901; 6 M113; 3 M106)
        3-4/3/GSR/B/124 MI (DS)
        3/A/3 ENG (CBT) (DS)
        SQUADRON TRAINS (-)

On 21 February 1991, after the last task force rehearsal and the TOC had halted and as the NCOs were setting up a small-arms test-

fire range, Command Sergeant Major Soucy arrived with an important passenger. In the back seat of his vehicle was Master Sergeant Cabrerra, a 2-4 Cav veteran who had departed the squadron in the summer of 1990 to attend the Sergeants Major Academy at Fort Bliss, Texas. While assigned to the squadron, he had served as the first sergeant of three of the troops at various times and as the operations sergeant major. He had just graduated from the academy and had found his way, by hook and crook, back to the squadron.

His saga is a complete story in itself. Suffice it to say that his arrival was due to the force of his personal energy and desire to return to his regiment in true cavalry tradition. I was skeptical at first of this old hand, but in short order, I knew that he would be a major actor in the scene that would shortly unfold. He immediately took a fresh look at our organization and preparation for combat.

The soldiers of TF 2-4 Cav's main command post. During one of the final rehearsals, the main CP came upon this tree in the desert. Since it is so unusual to see a tree of this size in the desert, we took this group picture.

The next day, he downloaded every vehicle in the TOC and had them repacked according to a load plan. We became bonded the second night he was with us when he, Sergeant First Class Fauver, and I spent all night putting acetate on the maps and then assembling them. He is a true warrior and I thank God that he arrived when he did. His fresh perspective assured a crew that had now been conducting combat operations for more than thirty days that all the little things were done. In short, he planned, executed, and supervised the most important precombat inspection of our lives.

The Plan

While the rest of the division focused much of its effort on planning for the offensive operation, TF 2-4 Cav was decisively engaged with the division's R&S operation. Consequently, the planning effort concentrated on command, control, and communications (C3) functions and other basic tactical issues essential to the operation. The task force leaders' largest challenge was to mold this non-doctrinal organization, with no two elements alike, into a cohesive unit with the teamwork necessary to accomplish the mission. Luckily, throughout the R&S mission, the task force had developed a way to work together and an understanding of the capabilities and limitations of each maneuver troop or company.

The task force followed the commanding general's guidance, which had been clearly stated at the division MAPEX on 13 and 14 February 1991:

1. Go north! "We are never coming back"; if you do not know what to do, keep moving north-on to the valley!
2. Rehearse at platoon level.
3. Verify who goes where and when.
4. Establish firm control of subordinate units at the line of departure.
5. Maintain an FM command net.
6. Move your rear boundaries as you move north.
7. Maintain ammunition discipline: do not fire at terrain, fire at the enemy!
8. Follow the order!

TF 2-4 Cav accomplished the mission. However, as is always the case, the plan and actual operations did not coincide. The operation was planned in five phases (see Table 4 and Maps 2, 3, 4, and 5). For planning purposes, H-hour was set for 0600 on G-day.

After Phase V was completed, depending on the mission, enemy, terrain, troops, and time available (METT-T), the task force would receive a FRAGO to execute any follow-on missions. The task force's

MAPEX focused on the tasks that would put the task force into the Euphrates River Valley oriented east toward Basra or through Phase IV. The squadron commander was confident that if the task force delivered the lead elements of the division into the Euphrates River Valley over the very difficult terrain, then it would have accomplished the lion's share of its mission. The commander focused on Phases II and III due to the uncertain enemy situation expected in Phases IV and V and because he felt the task force's main task was to lead.

Since the task force was to lead the division's main effort into the Euphrates River Valley, the command group spent time making sure it understood the CENTCOM commander's intent at the operational level. A thoughtful analysis of the commander in chief's intent, combined with the understanding of the division commander's intent, was critical to the task force's ability to accomplish the mission. More important for the leaders of the task force, this analysis would lead the task force to where we thought we would fight the enemy. The results of the R&S phase clearly showed that the Iraqis were not defending in our sector. Also, just prior to G-day, the SCO and the air troops of the squadron flew 100 kilometers into Iraq to conduct a route reconnaissance. They met no enemy resistance or observed any enemy activity.

Considering the "big picture" and understanding the division commander's intent allowed us to make some judgments as to where the task force would engage the enemy. In addition, best-case and worst-case scenarios were developed. In the best-case situation, the task force would move rapidly with little or no enemy contact into the Euphrates River valley, thereby cutting off the majority of the Iraqi combat forces between the division and Kuwait and allowing the VII Corps to destroy the majority of the mechanized force. In this event, the primary threat would be from dismounted infantry units, any possible reinforcements sent down Highway 8 from Baghdad, and any remnants that had escaped the VII Corps. In this case, TF 2-4 Cav could encounter some Iraqi mechanized forces as they attempted to retreat toward Baghdad.

Table 4. TF 2-4 Cav's Operations Plan (OPLAN)
Phase I
1200, G-4: Execute relief in place and turn over the security zone to the brigades in the sector. Occupy TAA Quarter and prepare for combat operations. Detach D/4 Cav to the 197th Brigade.

Phase II
2359, G-1: Conduct a route reconnaissance of Combat Trail Yankee to occupy area of operations (AO) Spur located approximately ten kilometers north of the border. On order, continue route reconnaissance to PL Lion (see Map 2).

Critical Tasks:

1900, G-1: Move from TAA Quarter to attack positions in the vicinity of Combat Trail Yankee and the Iraqi border intersection.

2359, G-1: Execute line of departure (LD).

0230, G-day: Move to PL Opus, approximately ten kilometers north of the border. Entire squadron (including combat trains) clears the LD. Upon A/13 FA's report that it is ready, execute PL Opus in squadron movement formation.

0430, G-day: Occupy AO Cav "A" along PL Colt and rearm and refuel.

0600, G-day (H-hour): Main body executes LD. TF 2-4 Cav executes PL Colt and continues reconnaissance mission to PL Lion.

1400, G-day: Conduct forward screen along PL Lion.

Phase III
On order, move to screen division's left flank forward of Combat Trail X-Ray in AO Saber from PL Jet to PL Viking. Guard left flank of 197th Brigade as it moves to Attack Position Kelly. Confirm Combat Trail X-Ray from PL Jet to PL Viking (see Map 3).

Critical Tasks:

Assist the forward passage of the 2d Brigade to seize Objective (Obj) Gray.

Receive attachment of D/4 Cav from 197th Brigade upon the 197th Brigade's closure on PL Lion.

Assist the forward passage of the 1st Brigade to Obj Red along Combat Trail Whiskey.

Collapse screen to center of the sector.

Move to occupy screen in AO Saber oriented northwest on Tallil Air Base.

Guard left flank of 197th Brigade as it moves to occupy Attack Position Kelly.

Phase IV

Guard left flank of 197th Brigade as it attacks to seize Battle Position (BP) 101 (see Map 4).

Critical Tasks:

    Establish contact with TF 2-69 Armor, the left flank unit of the 197th Brigade.

    Occupy successive battle positions to maintain contact with 197th Brigade and destroy any enemy forces threatening the flank of the 197th Brigade.

Phase V

Establish contact with the 2d Brigade at BP 103. Screen southern flank of 2d Brigade while it attacks to seize Obj Orange (Jalibah Air Base). Establish contact with 3d Armored Cavalry Regiment (3 ACR) to the south (see Map 5).

Critical Tasks:

    Collapse Phase IV screen.

    Occupy a task force rally point in the center of sector.

    Establish contact with 2d Brigade and the 3 ACR.

In the worst-case scenario, the Iraqi center of gravity, the elite Republican Guard divisions, would identify the division's move to cut them off early enough in the fight to conduct coordinated counterattacks to the west toward Baghdad. Here, the task force would be in for a real fight as early as the division's Obj Red. The CENTCOM commander in chief's intent was to cut off the Republican Guards divisions. Once these divisions realized that they were cut off, they would begin to move toward Baghdad. They would then be caught on the move and destroyed by the U.S. VII Corps, the theater main effort. In this case, the 24th Division and TF 2-4 Cav would encounter the remnants of the Republican Guards divisions that had not been destroyed by VII Corps, any reinforcements from Baghdad, any dismounted infantry units and rear area troops caught in the middle, and small units attempting to escape.

As it turned out, the operational objective was accomplished as the best of the best-case scenario. The XVIII Airborne Corps, lead by the 24th Division, cut off the Iraqi forces. The Republican Guards

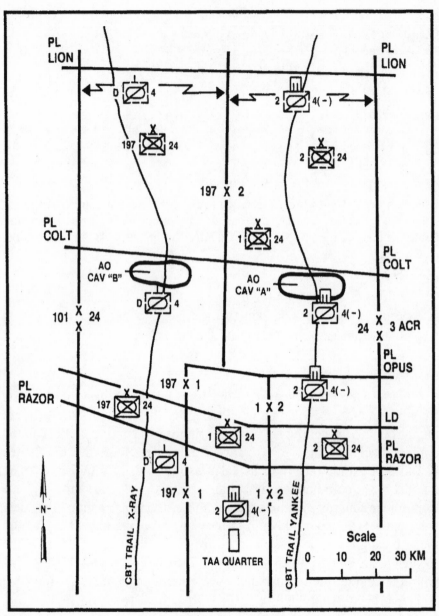

Map 2. Phase II

NOTE: This map is presented as a course-of-action sketch to visually depict the scheme of maneuver. It is not intended to be an accurate map.

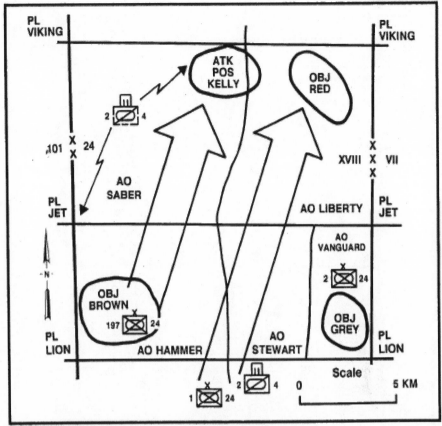

Map 3. Phase III

NOTE: This map is presented as a course-of-action sketch to visually depict the scheme of maneuver. It is not intended to be an accurate map.

divisions did not attempt a coordinated breakout, and the VII Corps destroyed them before they were able to conduct an organized withdrawal. Once the 24th Division blocked Highway 8, it turned east toward Basra to complete the destruction of the Iraqi Army in the Kuwaiti theater of operations.

Of course, as the sun came up on 23 February, the task force leaders knew none of this and they prepared for the worst-case situation. We had a good plan, were confident in our leadership, and had tremendous confidence in the soldiers and the task force. We had proven ourselves during the R&S phase and had rehearsed. The plan was complete and the leaders briefed their soldiers one last time. The task force prepared to attack north to the Euphrates.

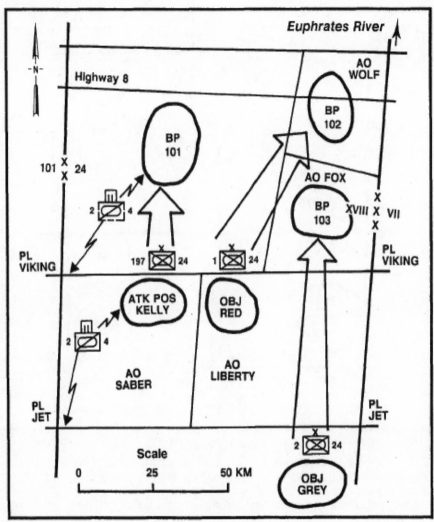

Map 4. Phase IV

NOTE: This map is presented as a course-of-action sketch to visually depict the scheme of maneuver. It is not intended to be an accurate map.

During the task force's command estimate process, it became apparent that because of the mission and the still almost unbelievable enemy situation that a revised movement technique would be required. The following factors compelled us to devise an unusual movement technique:

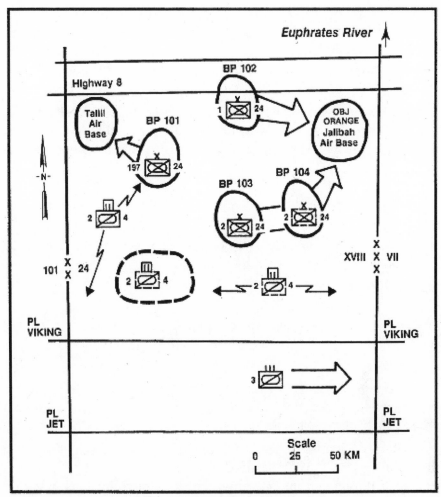

Map 5. Phase V

NOTE: This map is presented as a course-of-action sketch to visually depict the scheme of maneuver. It is not intended to be an accurate map.

• *Land navigation:* The task force only had global positioning systems (GPSs) down to the platoon level. Therefore, any section movement without GPSs was forbidden. Since our mission analysis revealed that, at least to PL Lion, our greatest threat was the terrain, the task force had to move with ground positioning devices. Also, most of our movement was to be at night, thus increasing the chances of miss-orientation. During the R&S operations, we discovered that one of the great dangers was to become miss-oriented, wander into another sector, and be mistaken for the enemy. Control was essential to prevent fratricide and control is a function of accurate situational awareness. In the desert, both control and situational awareness are based on knowing your exact location, which can only be obtained through the use of a GPS.

- *Security*: Since the task force was to lead the main effort by at least six hours, it had to move with definite front and rear boundaries. A definite rear boundary was critical to ensure that the task force did not intermingle with the follow-on task forces. Also, since TF 2-4 Cav would be in front and out of easy support range from the 2d Brigade, it had to have the combat power of the tank company within close supporting distance of the lead troop.

- *Indirect fire support*: The MLRS battery had to move with the main body but, because of its minimum range, be at least eight kilometers to the rear. The MLRS battery had to be protected by the main body.

- *Logistics*: Because of the planned refueling halts required within the first twenty-four hours, the combat trains also had to move with and be protected by the main body.

- *Command and control*: While moving, the task force had to be controlled by the TOC. Therefore, task force units had to remain within FM range of each other.

After considering all of these factors, the movement formation shown in Figure 1 was rehearsed. In fact, the task force used this technique throughout the operation with few modifications based on METT-T.

This movement formation is similar to the Soviet-style advance-guard formation. The Soviet advance-guard battalion is led by a combat reconnaissance patrol (CRP), which is usually a motorized rifle platoon that may be reinforced with chemical or engineer reconnaissance forces. Next is the forward security element (FSE), consisting of a motorized rifle company reinforced with tanks, artillery, mortars, engineers, and chemical defense.

The FSE advances at maximum speed and engages any lead enemy elements. "Through use of its mobility and firepower, it will seize and retain a line for formation subsequent commitment of the advanced guard's main body."[14] In this analogy, TF 2-4 Cav was both the CRP and FSE, while the 2d Brigade was the main force. The only exception was that our CSS assets were moved with the task force's main body.

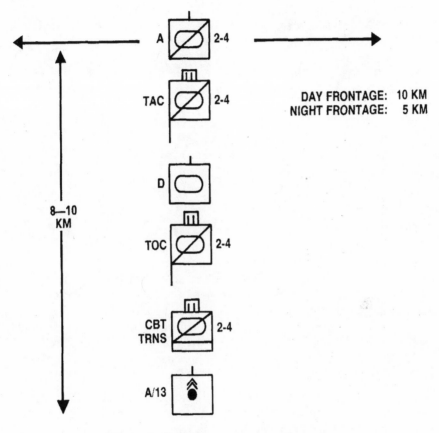

Figure 1. Task force movement formations

A LORAN (long-range navigation) global positioning system attached to the side mirror of a HMMWV. These systems were used extensively by the combat service support soldiers because of a higher probability of navigational errors. The reason was not because of the technology but because the device read in latitude/longitude as opposed to the military grid system. In order to move from point A to point B, the operator would get the grid, transpose it to a 1:250,000-scale map, read a military grid from the 1:250,000-scale map, transpose it back to latitude/longitude, enter it into the LORAN, and move out.

In essence, the device got you into the right area, which was good enough in the daytime because observation was good. On moonless nights, however, it was so dark that a soldier could be ten feet from a vehicle and not see it. Also, soldiers were serious about light discipline, so "hints" were hard to come by. Notice that no antenna is showing. Many industrious soldiers would run WD-1 communications wire from the LORAN to the external radio antenna, which increased the signal receptiveness.

VIII. THE EXECUTION OF THE BATTLE

At 1700, 22 February 1991, Major Barto, TF 2-4 Cav's executive officer, received a message from Major Holton, the executive officer of the 2d Brigade, stating that the operation was a "go." The operations plan was now an operations order with H-hour established as 0600, 25 February 1991. TF 2-4 Cav's mission was to execute Phase II of Operation Desert Storm at 1900, 24 February, which was a revised time for the lead elements to cross the berm into Iraq as the advanced guard of the 2d Brigade. (For clarity, it should be noted that the CENTCOM G-day was 23 February 1991, but the 24th Infantry Division (Mechanized) was not scheduled to execute its attack until G+1 or 25 February 1991.)

Earlier at 1500 on 22 February, TF 2-4 Cav received a mission from the 2d Brigade to conduct a zone reconnaissance to PL Colt at 1900 with one ground cavalry troop and the MLRS battery in support of the 2d Brigade reconnaissance and security plan. By this time, the division had conducted cross-border reconnaissance out to PL Lion with no enemy contact. Therefore, the commanding general decided to expand the division's security zone to PL Opus with elements of TF 2-4 Cav to facilitate movement during the actual attack. The task force commander requested permission to occupy PL Opus with the entire task force in order to assume the proper position in front of the 2d Brigade.

Permission was granted to conduct a reconnaissance in force to PL Colt but to return south of PL Opus with the maximum of one troop, the MLRS battery, and the necessary CSS assets. Therefore, A Troop, A/13 FA (MLRS), the TAC CP, and a CSS slice departed TAA Quarter at 1600 on 23 February to occupy the attack position by 1730. At 1800, A Troop linked up with TF 1-64 Armor for final coordination to conduct a forward passage of lines into Iraq. As part of the 2d Brigade's R&S plan, A/2-4 Cav, A/13 FA (MLRS), and the squadron TAC CP crossed the berm at 1900 (becoming the first ground units in the division to cross into Iraq) and conducted a zone reconnaissance oriented along Combat Trail Yankee.

Throughout the night, A Troop cleared the zone to PL Charger, while A/13 FA occupied firing positions in the vicinity of AO Spur, about eight kilometers north of the border along Combat Trail Yankee.

The squadron TAC CP controlled the operation while collocated with A/13 FA in AO Spur. No contact was made with the enemy. The support platoon(-) was collocated with A/13 FA and when A Troop returned to AO Spur, it refueled. At daylight, the support platoon(-) returned to the combat trains and continued on to the 224th BSA for resupply. The critical fuel resupply assets were at the BSA, which was located another forty kilometers to the rear of TAA Quarter.[15]

Into Iraq! The traditional "Welcome" sign is erected on the berm marking the Iraqi border.

As a standard operating procedure, the MLRS battery was always placed well forward to give the lead elements direct support fires. The commanding general's specific guidance was clear: "Never operate out of the FA umbrella and indirect fire is the weapon of choice." While the addition of the MLRS battery to the task force organization caused concern in the artillery community, its positioning in effect extended the division commander's area of operations twenty-five kilometers forward of the most forward ground element in the division.

Since we thought it would be a race to the Euphrates and Highway 8 to cut off the Iraqi Republican Guards divisions from escaping north to Baghdad, this extra twenty-five kilometers could be significant. In essence, the task force could attack the Iraqis with tremendous firepower with relatively little combat forces forward. Thus, the logic of placing the MLRS battery with the task force was justified.

As the execution time came closer and closer, I sensed a resolve throughout the TOC. Even though our team had been together for less than thirty days, we felt as if we had known each other forever. As I started to collect my thoughts for the most difficult speech of my life, I tried to picture myself as the lowest private in the TOC, and I asked myself what he would want to know before joining the battle. I knew my troopers were ready, yet it was my task to give them that final mental and emotional boost that, hopefully, would carry them through to the end. I knew they were thinking the same thoughts that I was-was I good enough? What was going to happen? What was going on around me? The soldiers' greatest fears were of the unknown.

The leaders knew the plan, but it was very important for everyone in the TOC to know it also. Therefore, as I gathered the troops together that morning for my final pitch, I began by using a rough terrain model and talked forty soldiers through our mission from start to finish (for the pre-attack situation, see Map 6). Then, in order to convey to this serious group that we were just a small part of a huge undertaking, I spent a few minutes explaining what I knew of the operation at the operational level. Finally, I told them how tremendously proud I was of them and that I knew they would all do their duty. I went on to say that we were a band of brothers and that each of us would depend on the other to accomplish the task at hand. We had all been training for the entire time we had been in the Army for this opportunity.

I told them to think back to every lesson they had ever learned in the Army, from their first day in basic training, and realize that they knew what to do. Now, it was just a matter of doing it. The next days would not be easy. When they looked at themselves in the mirror every day for the rest of their lives, I wanted them all to be proud of the person they saw.

I concluded with this thought, "All I want from each of you is ten days of stone-cold soldiering and we will be all right." Luckily, I was right, and every soldier I took into combat that day came out alive. With that, the NCOs conducted the final precombat inspection. Battle buddies checked each other over very carefully and we mounted our vehicles and moved north-to Iraq!

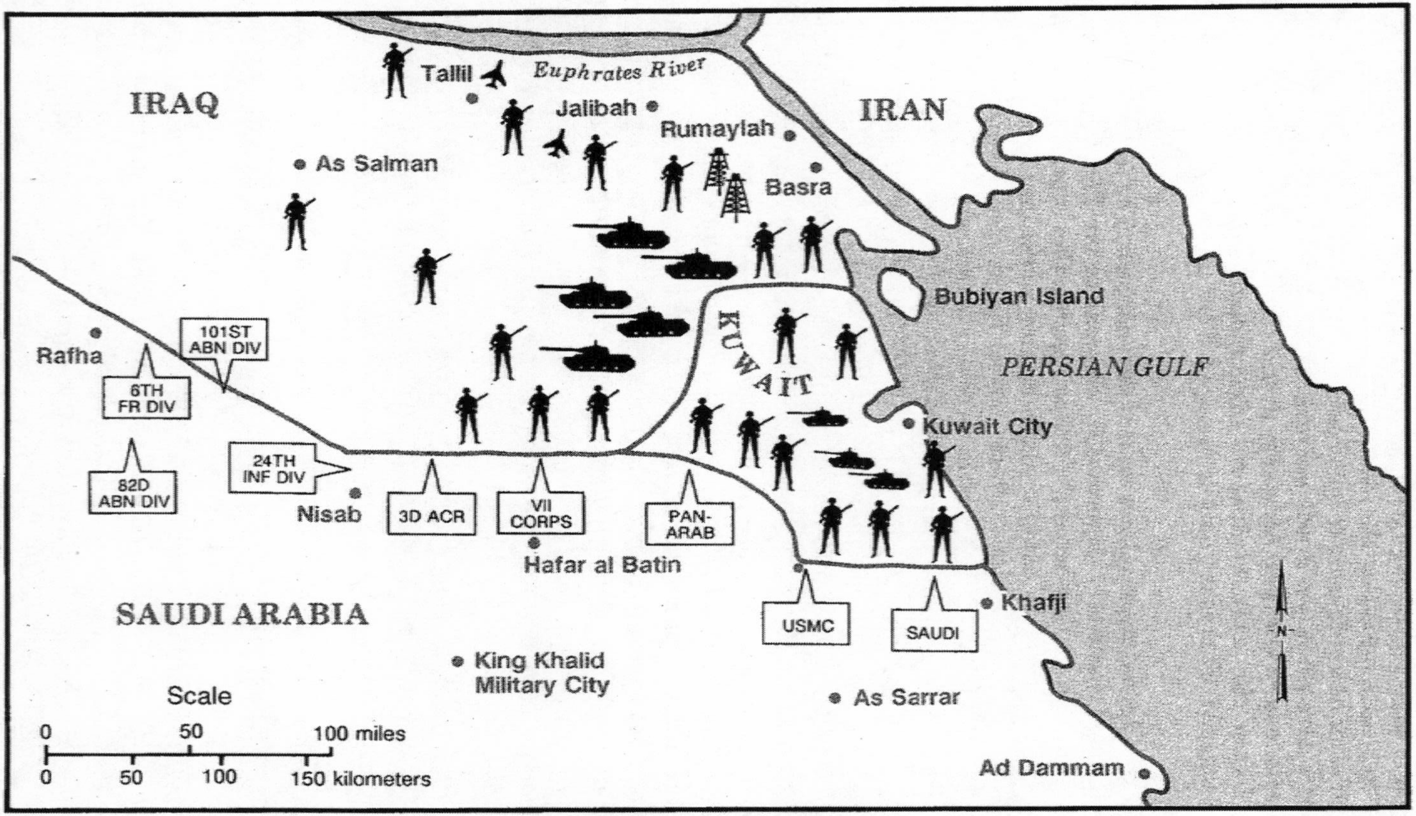

Map 6. Preattack situation

1100-1800, 24 February 1991

The TOC received a FRAGO from the 2d Brigade at 1100, 24 February:

"EXECUTE ASAP. LINK UP WITH SQUADRON(-) VICINITY AO SPUR AND ATTACK NORTH" (see Map 7).

The SCO ordered the task force to Readiness Condition (REDCON) 1. The SCO ordered A Troop to move out and A/13 FA to hold its position until the rest of the task force closed on AO Spur. The SCO instructed the SXO to move the remainder of the task force forward as quickly as possible and to assume the movement technique that had been rehearsed.

The SXO issued the execute order to D/3-69Armor, A/3 Engr(-), the squadron TOC, and the combat trains, all of which were still at TAA Quarter. Upon receipt of the order, the S4 notified the SXO that the fuel section(-) had not returned from resupplying at the BSA. The SXO gave the S4 permission to wait for the fuel assets and then to depart the assembly area as soon as possible. D/3-69 Armor, A/3 Engr(-), and the squadron TOC departed TAA Quarter at 1200. The combat trains awaited the return of the class III section and then departed at 1430.

The SCO pushed A Troop out along Combat Trail Yankee with the squadron TAC CP. D/3-69 Armor moved quickly, bypassed A/13 FA, and caught up with A Troop. Meanwhile, the TOC closed behind the tank company and A/13 FA fell in behind the TOC. When this maneuver was accomplished, the task force assumed the planned movement technique they had rehearsed several times earlier at TAA Quarter (during the night and day).

The task force executed the attack along Combat Trail Yankee, with the exception of the combat trains, which did not catch up in time. Consequently, the task force never really stopped at AO Spur, but because of the many rehearsals at TAA Quarter, all elements still were able to fall into their positions smoothly as the task force moved up Combat Trail Yankee. As the afternoon progressed, visibility turned from bad to worse. At 1200, visibility was about one kilometer; by 1400, when the TOC crossed the berm into Iraq, the visibility was only 200 meters. The combat trains crossed the berm at dusk under even more restricted visibility conditions.

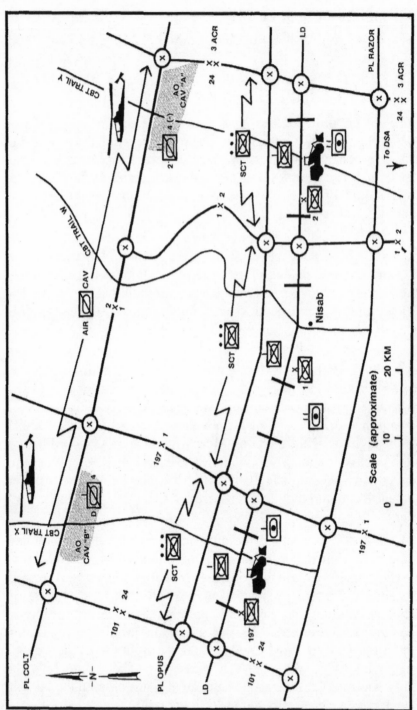

Map 7. Line of departure on G-day

At 1600, in accordance with the plan, an engineer platoon (which followed A Troop) began marking the route of march with a series of engineer stakes with chemlites attached. As nightfall approached, this marking technique proved invaluable in facilitating command and control and the rapid movement of the follow-on forces--especially the combat trains, which had limited land navigational aids or global positioning systems. By using this technique, the SCO emphasized control over security.

By 2000, the squadron had attacked through PL Colt, which was thirty-six kilometers north of the LD, and pushed forward to PL Lion. There was no enemy contact and the combat trains had not caught up with the movement formation. By this time, the main body of the 2d Brigade had passed the LD and was moving rapidly. This caused the combat trains some difficulty in closing on the rest of the task force because the primary route was now crowded with the 2d Brigade's combat team in attack formation.

The weather was clear as we formed the TOC and fell into formation behind Captain Steve Haag and his engineer company headquarters. The tank company was in front of him. Almost immediately, the sand started to blow and by the time we crossed the berm into Iraq, visibility was down to 200 meters. Several kilometers into Iraq, the TOC became intermixed with lead mechanized task forces of the 2d Brigade. Vehicle commanders were wildly waving at the tanks and Bradleys to let us through. I wondered how, in such a big desert, everyone could want to be in the same place.

By nightfall, we had broken free of the 2d Brigade's units and were closely following the chemlite trail left by the engineers. In combat, soldiers pay attention to what is going on around them, and especially, they concentrate on the vehicle they are following. We made several short stops to establish communications with all of our elements and to send messages to the division via the TACSAT radio. Then, I announced "jump it" and moved out, knowing everyone was behind me. As night fell, the fear of being left alone in the desert was almost worse than being in contact with the enemy.

1800, 24 February-0430, 25 February 1991

During Phase II of the operation, the task force conducted a zone reconnaissance along Combat Trail Yankee (see Map 8). Soon after

G-day weather conditions. This picture was taken just before crossing the berm into Iraq. This is definitely "no fly" weather.

crossing the LD, it became clear that the area was not defended. Therefore, the task force moved forward rapidly to exploit the element of surprise. Because of the significantly greater consumption of fuel by the M1A1 Abrams tanks over the M3A1 Bradleys, the entire task force refueled once on the move. The Abrams, however, had to refuel two additional times during the first twenty-four hours. The squadron commander quickly recognized the fuel constraint and conducted the future refueling operations with the forward momentum of the force.

The task force's mission was to clear the route and establish contact with the enemy. With every hour passing of no contact, the commander was impelled to keep moving as quickly as possible to exploit the success. To maintain the tempo and remain refueled, the SCO changed the organization of the task force, reorganizing A Troop and D/3-69 Armor into combination tank and scout platoons, which allowed the task force to refuel sequentially and still maintain momentum.

For example, one tank platoon was refueled when half full of fuel, and then it moved rapidly to catch up with A Troop, replacing one of its tank platoons. The replaced platoon then occupied a laager at the next refueling site while waiting for the fuelers to catch up;

A quick "comfort" break. The commander of the cavalry fighting vehicle gives the high sign and it's back on the road again.

then it refueled. Consequently, the task force never stopped. Earlier, the task force had rehearsed several refueling techniques in the TAA and all refueling operations were executed smoothly with the maximum number of hoses pumping at every site. These rehearsals significantly increased the speed of the task force's tempo during the attack.

Fuel was the primary concern of the task force as it continued to attack over long distances. Because of the M1A1 tanks' turbine engines, they required refueling every six hours regardless of the miles traveled. To conserve as much fuel as possible, the troop commanders implemented an innovative technique that significantly increased the sustainability of the tanks. Because enemy contact was light, the troop commanders surged their tanks forward at a high rate of speed to predesignated linkup points along the route. Once the tanks arrived at the linkup points, they would shut down, to conserve fuel and wait for the arrival of the M3A1 and M113A2 vehicles.

When enemy contact was likely, the troop commanders reverted to their normal tactical movement formations. Significant during this fast-moving phase of the operation was the fire support officer's (FSO's) constant coordination of the fire support coordination line (FSCL). The coordination of fires between the rear of the task force and forward edge of the lead task forces of the maneuver Troopers brigades was always a great concern. The constant shifting of the

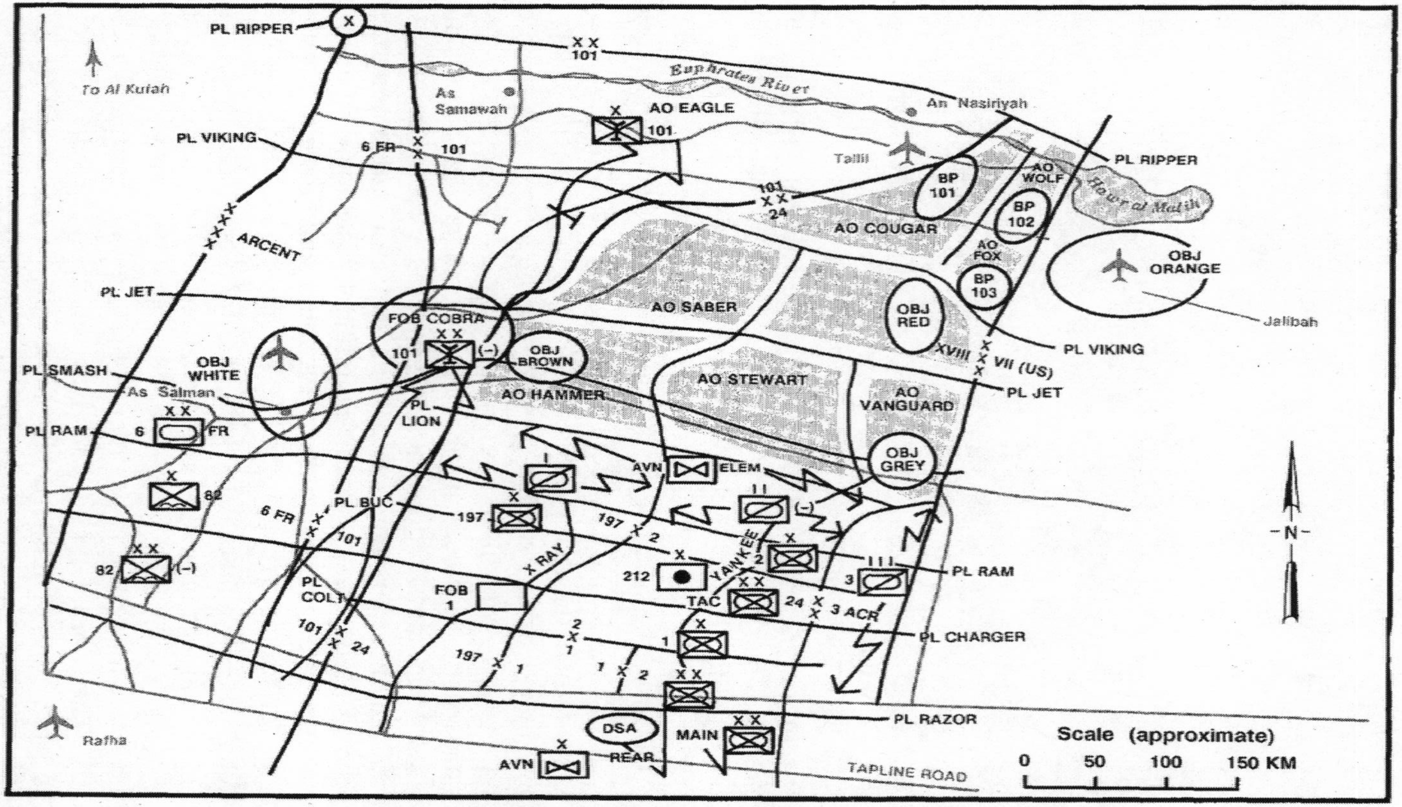

Map 8. Attack to Phase Line Lion

FSCL as the formation moved forward and the spacing between the reconnaissance force and the lead maneuver task forces had to be continuously monitored. Even though no indirect fires were used during this phase, coordination was constantly effected throughout the movement. At the same time, the corps was adjusting the restrictive firing line (RFL) to our front. The entire leadership monitored the movement of the corps RFL, because the task force was responsible for an ever-increasing area to the front.

By adjusting its movement based on the evolving enemy situation and by pressing forward as rapidly as the logistics allowed, the task force accomplished its mission of assisting the rapid attack of the 2d Brigade. The 2d Brigade was the division's main effort and TF 2-4 Cav facilitated the brigade's movement to PL Lion by identifying the high-mobility corridors in the sector.

We moved all night long and the TOC pulled into position around 0430, attacking over 160 kilometers in about 17 hours. Our anxiety levels started to increase because we knew that today we would fight. As it turned out, we did not fight that day. Since we had had no enemy contact, the enemy probably did not know how far we had come. We felt that if we pressed the attack, it would surely surprise the Iraqis as we proceeded toward the river.

Next, we quickly set up the TOC and reported to higher headquarters via TACSAT radio. Then, I turned the TOC over to the battle captain and fell asleep in the front seat of my HMMWV. An hour later, the SCO woke me; the task force was conducting refueling operations. I went back to the TOC and the SC Owent to sleep next to the vehicles.

As the morning progressed, more and more vehicles were moving around us. At about 0900, Major Arnold Smith, executive officer, 3-41 FA, part of the 2d Brigade combat team, came in the TOC and asked if he could have some fuel (since the TOC was refueling at the time). We gave him some diesel and he left. As it turned out, many units had become miss-oriented the previous night and had spent most of the morning sorting themselves out, thus explaining all the vehicle movement. We made sure that these vehicles did not pass us to the north because the task force was the farthest northern unit in the division.

Troopers from A Troop taking a break during their dash north. Notice the chemical protective over garments, which were worn by all the troopers of the 24th Division. They donned the suits on the first day of the air war and removed them when they redeployed into Saudi Arabia at the end of the ground war. Troopers wore the bulky and filthy suits for over two months.

0430-1200, 25 February 1991

In the original division plan, the task force was to consolidate along PL Lion and regain control of D/4 Cav while the division paused for twenty-four hours. This pause allowed the CSS assets to establish forward support areas and resupply the division along PL Lion. However, because of the lack of enemy contact, the division commander ordered the 1st Brigade to assume the main effort and attack at 1400. Meanwhile, TF 2-4 Cav was to protect the northwestern flank of the 1st Brigade as it attacked to seize Obj Red.

At 0630, the executive officer requested that the 2d Brigade commander release control of the task force to the 1st Brigade. The 2d Brigade commander approved the request via FM radio. The executive officer immediately entered the 1st Brigade FM command net, rendered a commander's situation report, and requested further instructions. The 1st Brigade had been moving north in the center of the division's sector and was located approximately thirty kilometers behind PL Lion. At the same time, TF 2-4 Cav had reconnoitered an easily traffic-able route up the escarpment, the significant terrain feature along PL Lion. The TF 2-4 Cav TOC reported the route to the 1st Brigade commander, who immediately moved his entire brigade along the identified route and deployed it along PL Lion. PL Lion was established as the LD for the 1st Brigade's attack to seize Obj Red.

Shortly after the operational control of TF 2-4 Cav was given to the 1st Brigade, the TOC contacted the 197th Brigade's TOC and requested that the D/4 Cav be detached from the 197th Brigade and attached to the TF 2-4 Cav. The commander of the 197th Brigade approved this request and a task force communications vehicles (RETRANS) station was dispatched to establish FM communications with the D/4 Cav. Upon attachment to TF 2-4 Cav, D/4 Cav was located in the division right zone approximately fifty kilometers from the 1st Brigade's attack position. Arriving about two hours later at 1100, D/4 Cav rapidly refueled.

While deployed along PL Lion, the task force again conducted refueling operations, which depleted 75 percent of the diesel fuel supplies in the combat trains. The S4 cross-leveled his fuelers and sent the empty fuelers to the nearest planned BSA (24th Forward Support Battalion [24 FSB]) to resupply. Because of the change in the plan and the deletion of the operational pause, the 24 FSB had not yet arrived at the planned BSA. As a result, the task force's fuel resupply convoy had a difficult time locating the resupply point (because of the task force's change of mission) and did not rejoin the combat trains full of fuel for over forty-eight hours.

The lack of a command and control capability and the limited number of position locating devices were major contributors to the confusion experienced by these critical CSS assets. If not for herculean efforts and innovative techniques by the S4, deputy commander, command sergeant major, and the HHT command group, the task force's attack into the Euphrates River Valley might have been more vulnerable to enemy counterattack.

Since the task force had never planned to conduct a moving flank guard mission, no rehearsal had been conducted and no standing operating procedures established. Therefore, the commander immediately called all the commanders into the TAC CP and executed a quick sand-table exercise. Then, the commander positioned the troops into the proper movement formations over the FM command net and

TF 2-4 Cav was deployed to protect the 1st Brigade's flank. When visibility permitted, it was incredibly awesome and encouraging to see the combat power displayed in the desert for as far as the eye could see. Formations could actually be executed in textbook or sand-table fashion.

briefed the new mission (see Figure 2).

At noon, I gave the command "jump it" and we moved down to assume our position as guard on the task force's flank. It was an impressive sight to look across the desert and see the 1st Brigade's combat team stretching as far as the eye could see. Visibility at this time was good, but again, within a few hours, visibility was reduced to less than a kilometer. At 1400, I had slept only two hours in the last thirty-two.

1400, 25 February-0200, 26 February 1991

At 1400, the 1st Brigade's commander, Colonel John LeMoyne, issued the attack order and the brigade executed the LD (PL Lion) to formation seize Obj Red (see Map 9). TF 2-4 Cav oriented on TF 4-64 Armor and maintained contact with them throughout the attack. During the attack, D/4 Cav made its first contact with the enemy, discovering and capturing four enemy prisoners of war (EPWs). They were quickly moved to the combat trains, where they were held until the squadron battlefield information coordinator (First Lieutenant Brian Edholm) and the interpreter were able to interrogate them at 2200 that night.

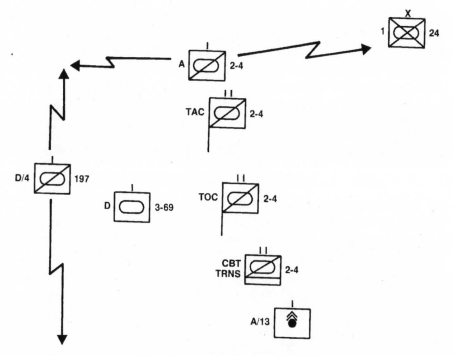

Figure 2. Flank guard formation

The Iraqi EPWs said that they were part of the early warning network along the Saudi Arabian-Iraqi border. During the initial assault, they had lost their commercial-type telephone communications and when they discovered the scope of the division's attack, they had run north and hidden until captured by D/4 Cav. They also reported that no significant Iraqi units were in the area. The EPWs were then evacuated to the collection point.[16]

Throughout the operation, the task force had a Kuwaiti national as its interpreter. His name was Waleed Y. "Wally" Al-Gharabally and he had been on a business trip to Bahrain when the Iraqis seized Kuwait. He volunteered to serve as an interpreter and joined the task force while it was at TAA Quarter just prior to the attack. His service was invaluable to the task force throughout the operation. One of the most important things Wally did was to monitor a short-wave radio he had brought with him and he regularly gave us updates as to how the overall war was going. Wally was the first to inform us that Kuwait City had been liberated.

Upon closure on Obj Red, fuel became critical. The class III section had not returned from resupply and the task force had just completed another long move. Again, decisive action was needed to find fuel. The DCO retraced our route to find any fuel assets. His search was productive and by 0900, 26 February, he had coordinated and delivered two 5,000 tankers from the 724th Main Support Battalion and one fuel HEMTT (heavy expanded mobility tactical truck) borrowed from 3-15 Inf for emergency resupply.

Additionally, the support platoon began filling a common ground and aircraft fuel (JP-4) from the forward area refuel point (FARP) HEMTTs into ground combat vehicles as an emergency resupply. Even though the task force had detached its air cavalry troops, it had kept the fuel resupply asset for emergency use for either aircraft or ground vehicles. Also, the task force was able to increase its fuel-carrying capacity by loading 500-gallon blivets of fuel onto the back of the engineer company's dump trucks. These aggressive and innovative techniques kept the task force operational for another twenty-four hours.[17]

After moving out on the flank guard mission, we drove like maniacs. The M1s and Bradley fighting vehicles easily traversed the terrain at about thirty kilometers per hour. The TOC in its M113-series wheeled vehicles were moving at top speed over very rough terrain in order to keep up with the Abrams tanks and Bradley fighting vehicles. As it turned dark and the drivers and vehicle commanders donned their PVS-7 night-vision goggles, I gave my driver clear instructions, "Don't lose that tank."

It was quite a ride, but the TOC did not lose a single vehicle from the formation. Also, as dusk fell, the GPS "blackout" window occurred, which made staying close to the combat vehicles even more pressing. "Blackout" periods occurred for about two hours a day when one of the three satellites required for operation fell under the horizon. Movement tended to slow considerably during the "blackouts." The LORAN systems, however, did not have "blackouts" because they were ground based.

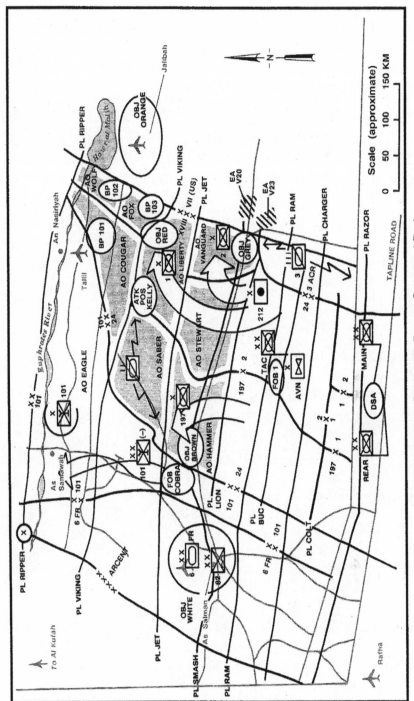

Map 9. Attack to Objectives Brown, Grey, and Red

-73-

With the task force arrayed in the flank guard formation, the squadron˙ executive officer **Major Barto** prepared to move out.

0200, 26 February-0400, 27 February 1991

At 0200, 26 February, the task force received a change in its mission from division via the TACSAT radio:

"SCREEN THE LEFT FLANK OF THE 197 BDE ALONG PL VIKING AND CONTINUE TO SCREEN THE LEFT FLANK DURING THE ATTACK TO SEIZE BATTLE POSITION 101" (see Maps 10 and 11).

At this point, the command relationship for the task force became difficult. While the task force was never officially attached to the 197th Brigade, it still was responsible for the flank security of the 197th Brigade (also under division control). The key point is that the task force was under division control, but it could not remain in constant communication with a division command post.

The task force ordinarily used the TACSAT radio to communicate with the division assault command post, but since the TACSAT was not mobile, there were extended periods of time when the task force was out of contact with the division's command posts and its FM radio lacked the required range. Despite these facts, an aggressive C3 system through the task force's TOC and TAC CP was able to maintain contact with

The squadron commander, **Lieutenant Colonel Thomas J. Leney**, thanks our Kuwaiti interpreter, Waleed Y. **"Wally" Ai-Gharabally**, who was a true soldier.

either the 197th Brigade or the division assault command post.

The task force's S2 section performed yeoman's work in monitoring the division's battle, which was now turning east, while the 197th Brigade was still driving north and maintaining contact with various units to keep the command group aware of the friendly and enemy situation. At this point in the battle, A/13 FA was returned to division artillery control.

At 0230, the SCO issued a FRAGO and the task force began executing its new mission. This scheme of maneuver placed D/4 Cav on the far left or northwest, A Troop on the right, and D/3-69 Armor in the center of the sector (in depth). That night, the wind picked up and by0300, it was blowing so hard that any movement was dangerous. In fact, individual troopers were knocked to the ground as they manned their units' perimeters. The wind and blowing sand were a bad omen for the next day's operations.

The dawn of 26 February broke almost unknown to any of the troopers of the task force. A blinding sandstorm had limited visibility to ten feet throughout the sector. As the lead unit, A Troop, moved out to secure the left flank of the 197th Brigade as it attacked to seize BP 101, its lead M3s were quickly mired to their fenders in wet muck

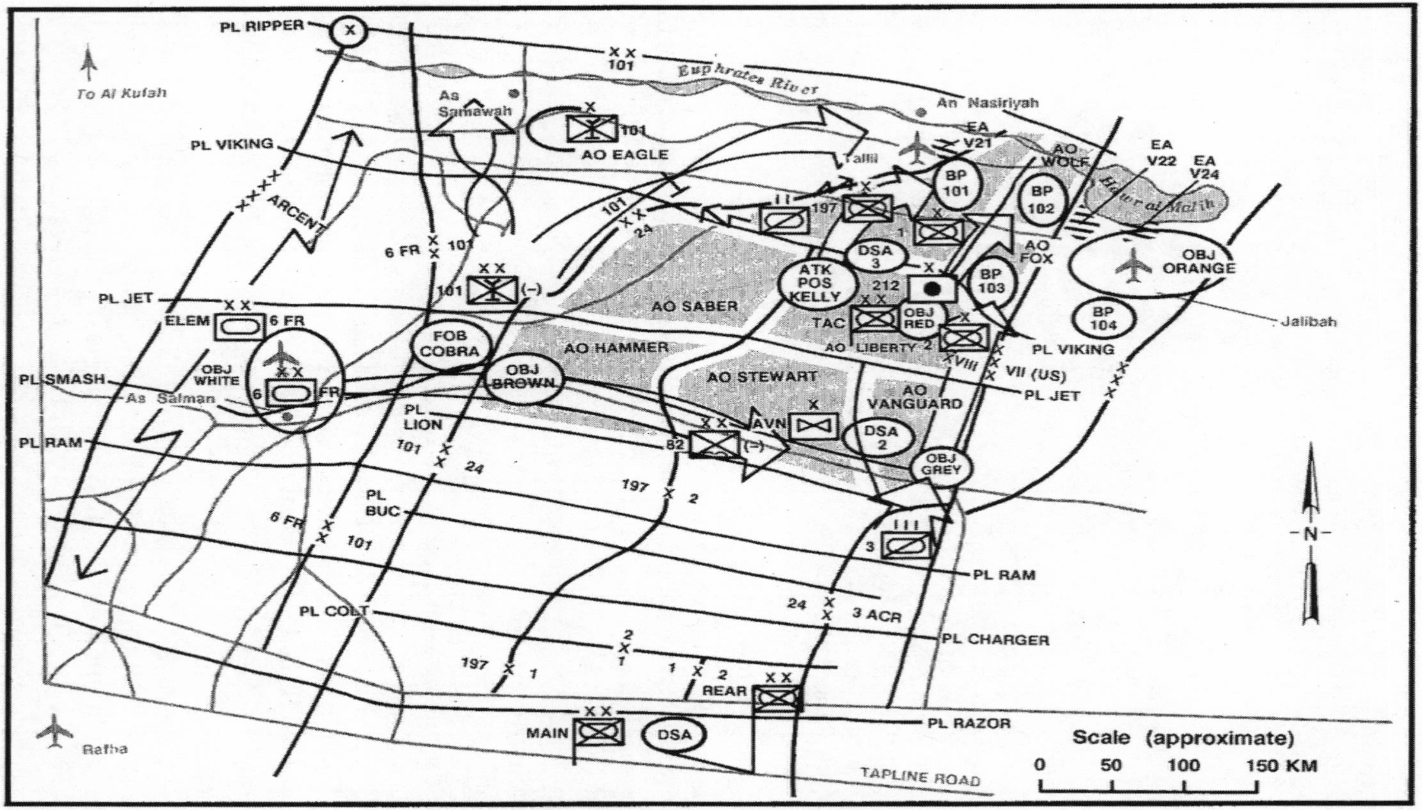

Map 10. Attack into the Euphrates River valley

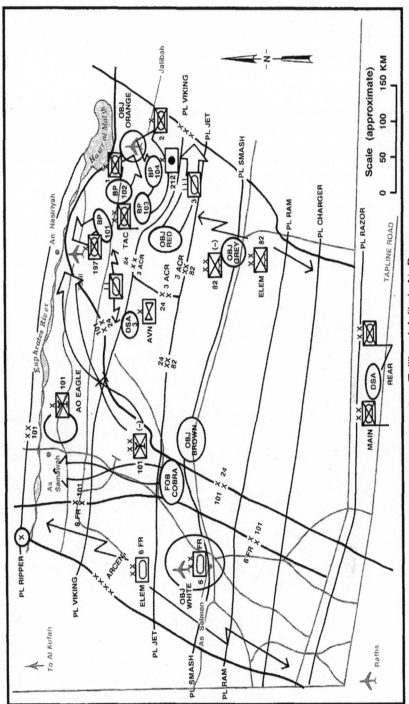

Map 11. Attack to Tallil and Jalibah Air Bases

-77-

and any attempt to move caused the M3s to sink deeper.

Further reconnaissance soon found that the flank was impassable to friendly or enemy forces. The lead tracked vehicles from A Troop moved blindly as they pushed out to occupy the screen line. Because of the zero-visibility conditions, they drove right into a large bog. The wind was blowing so hard that it covered the ground with a fine dust that disguised the traffic-ability of the ground below. Two M88s and two armored combat engineer (ACE) vehicles were soon badly mired as they attempted to recover the M3s.

At 0300, the SCO arrived at the TOC and I gave him a report on the fuel resupply situation. It looked bleak. The SCO directed me to get some sleep. Just outside the TOC, the troopers had erected our A-frame tent in the raging wind and sandstorm. They staked it down from every angle and I fell down on a cot to sleep. For some reason, I could not fall asleep. As the wind buffeted the tent, it gave me an eerie feeling.

Giving up the idea of sleep, I stood up just as Master Sergeant Cabrerra entered the tent. He asked me where I was going and I told him I could not sleep and was going back to the TOC. He reminded me of the SCO's directive to sleep and right at that time a gust of wind lifted the entire tent off the ground, leaving Cabrerra and me lying on the ground sure that if we were not dead, we were at least mortally wounded. After counting fingers and arms and ensuring that every thing worked, I retired to the friendly front seat of my HMMWV for a couple hours sleep. As I fell asleep, all I could think of was the message my wife would get, "We regret to inform you that your husband was killed by a runaway tent."

The TOC reported the impassable area to the division via TACSAT radio, while the TAC CP communicated by FM to the brigade and its lead task forces. Unfortunately, because of the extremely limited visibility, elements of the lead task forces of the 197th Brigade also became mired. However, the task forces reports allowed the 197th Brigade to modify the concept of the operation from two task forces abreast to a column of task forces. The sparse enemy situation and extremely poor visibility allowed the 197th Brigade to seize BP 101 easily while husbanding its combat power.

Even in open desert, land navigation was sometimes difficult because of the large **wadis**. The biggest problem with land navigation devices is that they give a straight-line azimuth, which disregards terrain features. This "Ranger"-style land navigation leads one to believe that the shortest way is the best way (which is often wrong). Notice the vegetation at the bottom of this wadi and the steepness of the slope. The water collects at the bottom of the wadis, causing vegetation to grow and vehicles to become mired in them.

This terrain was particularly treacherous on moonless nights while using land navigation aids. Because of little ambient light, the moonless nights in the desert were the darkest black imaginable. Darkness combined with the poor depth perception of night observation devices caused vehicle drivers to drive into the wadis.

Once at BP 101, the 197th quickly reorganized and conducted an armored raid that neutralized Tallil Airfield. TF 2-4 Cav's efforts for the next eighteen hours were to recover its vehicles from the bog, conduct badly needed refueling operations, and reorganize on the high ground running along PL Viking.

0400-1200, 27 February 1991

At 0400, 27 February, the task force received a change of mission:

"MOVE BEHIND 197 BDE AND BLOCK HIGHWAY 8 ORIENTED WEST. ASSIST THE MOVEMENT OF THE 197 BDE AS THEY FOLLOW THE 1ST AND 2ND BDE ATTACKING TO THE EAST."

The first task was to re-consolidate the task force and prepare for future operations. While the battle staff developed the courses of action to accomplish the new mission, the SCO and SXO issued the following order to regroup:

- Complete re-consolidation on high ground south of PL Viking.
- Consolidate recovery teams in the bog, leave local security, and report location.
- Move to designated TAA and report when ready for future operations.

Shortly thereafter, the SXO briefed the SCO, who approved the following scheme of maneuver. TF 2-4 Cav left one platoon and the squadron maintenance technician at the bog to continue recovery operations. Meanwhile, the bulk of the task force moved to the east around the bog and occupied the designated blocking position along Highway 8 with two troops abreast and one troop in depth.

Once the plan was approved, the critical task was to consolidate the task force and regain the ability to move rapidly around the battlefield. Therefore, the TOC moved to a TAA located well clear of the bog area and would brief the troop commanders as they arrived en route to the blocking position.

The troops began their movement. The TOC moved to the TAA, reentered the division's TACSAT net, and rendered a situation report to the division G3 at the assault CP. The division G3 canceled the previous mission to occupy blocking positions and issued a new FRAGO. By this time, the division situation had turned into a classic exploitation operation that was moving very rapidly to the east toward Basra.

Consequently, the division's previous concept to utilize the squadron in an economy-of-force mission on the division's western flank had been overcome by events. Therefore, the division G3 changed the task force's mission and ordered it to move east as quickly as possible behind the 1st Brigade as the division reserve.

"Jump it!" The TOC was on the move again. We knew that the division was in the Euphrates River Valley and that we were not far behind. The delay at the bog had put the task force behind the rest of the division and we had to get moving to catch up! The weather had finally cleared and we observed many helicopters operating in the area. For the first time, we saw Bedouins in their camps as we drove by. They did not seem concerned and we were astounded by their

miserable living conditions.

The terrain for the first time looked like the desert from the Lawrence of Arabia movie. Huge drifts of soft sand made all vehicle movement difficult. Our first major crisis in the TOC occurred at this time. HQ 30, the M577 that was the heart of the TOC, broke down. We quickly hooked it up to another M577 and towed it to the TAA, where we set up. Luckily, it was only a short distance, because the second M577 began to overheat because of its load and the soft sand.

A quick examination of HQ 30 revealed that it could not be fixed quickly. However, we could not operate effectively without it and we had to consider where the six soldiers, including a Stars and Stripes reporter, were going to ride if we had to leave it. Master Sergeant Cabrerra and I tried to figure out a solution.

Luck was with us that day, for who pulled up right behind us about that time – the combat trains. We bolted for the trains, knowing that we did not have time to fix the HQ 30. While we were scrambling, the task force was moving farther and farther ahead of us.

When we got to the combat trains, we found Master Sergeant Stewart, the squadron motor sergeant, looking frazzled with a large black cigar clenched between his teeth. After we gave him a quick explanation, he shook his head as only an old motor sergeant could and waved his hand toward an M3A1 with a fire control problem. The answer was clear. We threw a tow bar on the Bradley and led it over to the beleaguered HQ 30, and within fifteen minutes, we were back on our way. This was the first time I had ever met Master Sergeant Stewart, and again, I knew I was making a great impression.

1200-2100, 27 February 1991

At 1200, 27 February 1991, the task force received another change of mission:

"MOVE ALONG HWY 8 BEHIND THE 1ST BDE TO OCCUPY ATAA. LINK UP WITH THE ASSAULT CP, REPORT ARRIVAL AND STAND BY FOR FUTURE MISSIONS" (see Map 12).

As fate would have it, the current task force FRAGO in effect was already moving the task force in the right direction, or east, and it

As the task force broke **into the Euphrates River Valley**, scenes of Bedouins tending their flocks were common. These people were virtually not fazed by the huge combat operations in progress. These nomads roamed the desert and had no real national allegiance. During the R&S phase, the task force conducted several operations to assist the Bedouins in clearing the division sector as they crossed into Saudi Arabia from Iraq. These borders meant little to them as their forebears had roamed the desolate wasteland for centuries.

was a simple task to continue moving the troops to the east.

By 1400, the task force was moving northeast toward the new TAA located on Highway 8. D/4 Cav was in the lead and A Troop and D/3-69 Armor followed. During this movement, the troopers of the task force moved through several large Iraqi supply and storage areas. It was also the troopers first look at the carnage of war. It was a sobering sight that hardened the determination of the troopers, as they had not yet been tested with close combat. They did not wait long for their first test.

As the task force overran these supply depots, elements of A/3 Engr began destroying high-value supplies. As they approached enemy positions, the soldiers were struck by the starkness of the Iraqi soldiers living conditions. For the most part, they lived in foxholes that were more flat than deep. Most holes were about three feet deep, with thinly constructed overhead covers and just large enough to hold one or two foam sleeping mats. All of their personal equipment was also stored in these holes. In fact, most of it was still present in the holes.

The element of surprise was apparent. Often, one would see within ten meters a row of strewn Iraqi equipment, including the soldier's weapon, helmet, web gear, and jacket left on the battlefield as the Iraqi soldier had obviously fled. The engineers discovered a brand-new American 2 1/2-ton truck that had been booby trapped with grenades. It was a sad sight when the engineers destroyed the truck and then mounted their terribly road-weary truck of the same model.

At 1600, the task force was closing on the new TAA. Also during this move, the task force encountered a large number of Bedouins along the route. Their living conditions were austere to say the least, but they did not appear interested or threatened by the movement of U.S. Forces. The task force moved rapidly through the area.

D/4 Cav arrived at the new assembly area first, crossed Highway 8, and assumed a defensive position overlooking a causeway over the southern most canal of the Euphrates River. At 1630, as D/4 Cav began to occupy its position in the TAA, it discovered a huge underground ammunition storage area protected by an Iraqi artillery battery equipped with self-propelled howitzers and antiaircraft guns. Elements of D/4 Cav took the enemy under fire and began to deploy.

While D/4 Cav was moving on the ammunition dump, four Iraqi tanks and one BMP appeared from the southeast and began moving toward the causeway at a range of 1,200 meters. The spot reporting of the incident was quick and accurate through squadron to division. The SCO requested close air support for the task force. The request was denied.

In the meantime, D/4 Cav destroyed the lead tank with direct fire and engaged the artillery battery with mortar fire. As the sun set, AH-64 attack helicopters were vectored in and destroyed the remainder of the column with missile fire. At the same time, the Iraqis in the ammunition storage area began to surrender en masse. They were joined by the survivors of the tank and BMP platoon, and all were moved to a holding area along Highway 8, where the task force's medics rendered medical aid to the wounded Iraqis.

An Iraqi bunker in the Euphrates River Valley along Highway 8. This bunker was less than three feet high and an Iraqi soldier's entire kit and a foam sleeping mat were found inside. Note the shallow fighting position in the foreground.

Bedouin women with a child, quickly took advantage of the generosity of the task force by taking food, water, and anything else left in the desert.

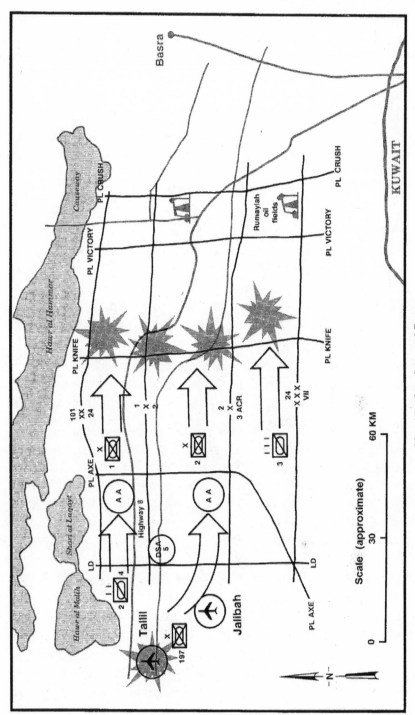

Map 12. Attack toward Basra

Clearly, the task force could not transport the EPWs to a designated holding area; therefore, this site was designated a task force EPW holding area and reported to division. The EPWs were provided food and water and told to remain in place. Later that evening, military police arrived and secured the site.[18]

During the firefight, the DCO contacted the TOC and reported that he was in bound with the support platoon's fuel HEMTTs. Since the task force was low on fuel, the leadership was relieved to regain contact with the support platoon. The DCO passed control of the fuel vehicles to the SXO, received a quick tactical update, and returned to find the field trains. The SXO established a refueling site within three kilometers of the fighting, which was still in progress.

While the squadron commander continued to fight the battle, the SXO left the TOC, moved to the refueling site, and established a linear formation site to allow for the fastest possible refueling operation. The SXO notified the SCO as soon as the site was established and the SCO ordered platoons to refuel and then return to their positions.

Incredibly, over the next two hours, in a textbook-style operation, the entire task force, to include the MLRS battery (which had been reattached) was completely fueled. By 2000, the task force was ready to continue combat operations and again entered the fray.

Fuel! For the last forty-eight hours, the TOC was consumed with obtaining it. Where was it? How much was there? How much did we have in the trains? Where was the support platoon? The battle captains were constantly talking to the troop commanders and getting updates as to their fuel status. The M3s were not a great concern, but the tanks required constant refueling. It seemed like every time we coordinated a refueling operation, the troop commander was back on the radio wanting to know where the next refueling site was.

The task force had just used the last of its emergency resupply of fuel. The emergency fuel was the aviation fuel from the FARP HEMTTs, which were kept with the task force trains in the event the air troops were reattached to the task force. The aviation fuel was the common fuel JP-4. During Desert Shield, the division had used this common fuel for both ground vehicles and aircraft, but it was discovered that long-term use would foul the vehicle engines. The

The task force arrives on Highway 8. The first significant enemy contact occurred shortly after this picture was taken.

task force's fuel situation was certainly in the management-by-exception category.

When I received the radio message from the DCO and the support platoon leader, First Lieutenant Bob Hamilton, I was elated. Finally, we could get this fuel bear off our backs. I asked him for their position and discovered that they were only ten kilometers to our rear. I directed them to move to an easily identifiable interchange on Highway 8 and to stand by.

I turned the TOC over to the battle captain and left to make the linkup with the precious fuel tankers. I personally decided to supervise the refueling operations because I knew we would soon receive another mission change to move to the east. The refueling had to be accomplished as rapidly as possible to facilitate this move and I saw this as a great opportunity to refuel the entire task force fast. I knew that a fully resupplied task force would give us another twenty-four hours or so of operations before we would have to launch the fuel HEMTTs again to find a fuel resupply point. Also, since I was determined not to lose control of the HEMTTs again, I wanted to issue instructions to the support platoon leader face to face and coordinate directly with the DCO.

On the way to the linkup point, I ran across Brigadier General Joe N. Frazar III, the ADC(S) (assistant division commander [support]) who was moving east on Highway 8. I flagged him down and told him not to go any farther east because the task force was still involved in the firefight just north of the highway. He thanked me for stopping him. I gave him a quick update and explained our fuel situation. He told me that a column of 5,000-gallon fuel tankers were en route to that spot as we spoke.

I started to feel better already and filed that information away for my briefing to the DCO and support platoon leader. I also called the S4 at the ALOC and gave him the welcomed news. Night was beginning to fall and Iraqis were wandering all over the area. We did not have time to dismount and control these enemy soldiers, so we ignored them as long as they continued to wave their white flags and stayed near the highway.

I linked up with the support platoon leader and led the platoon to the refueling site located close to the troops, but still secure from the firefight still in progress. Upon arriving, I reported to the SCO that we were ready to pump gas. Immediately, he began to direct units to withdraw from their fighting positions and refuel. I stayed at the refueling site until the last platoon had arrived and then returned to the TOC. The entire operation had been accomplished in two hours.

During this period, I was confronted with two situations that will remain with me forever. The first filled me with pride and the second amused me. As I pulled onto Highway 8, I saw several dead Iraqi soldiers scattered over the area where several trucks had been destroyed. One dead Iraqi lay right in the middle of the highway and was covered with a black plastic trash bag so common to the American soldier.

I realized that an unnamed American soldier, after having killed the Iraqi soldier, had the compassion to cover the body before moving on. I was overcome with pride for my comrades in arms. Some soldier, in conducting this very serious and deadly business of war, had maintained his respect for life by paying an enemy soldier this small tribute of covering his dead body.

The second incident was on the lighter side. On returning to the TOC, Master Sergeant Cabrerra pulled me to the side in a very serious manner and informed me of an incident involving Iraqi EPWs. While I was at the refueling site, the TOC crew had rounded up several small groups of Iraqi soldiers who had been wandering around in the vicinity of the highway. In order to gain some combat information, Wally,

The task force arrives on Highway 8. The first significant enemy contact occurred shortly after this picture was taken.

our Kuwaiti interpreter, accompanied the battlefield information co-ordinator, First Lieutenant Brian Edholm, to interrogate these EPWs.

On seeing the Iraqi soldiers, Wally became very emotional, angry, and hostile. Wally launched into these dazed EPWs with a vengeance, and though Cabrerra could not understand a word of his harangue, he knew it was not complimentary. This mild-mannered Kuwaiti businessman vented the frustration he had pent up since the previous August when these now cowering soldiers had invaded his country. While Wally was not gaining a lot of information, the TOC security crew found his emotional outburst rather amusing until he turned to Cabrerra and asked for a gun so he could execute these "dogs" where they sat. Cabrerra immediately escorted Wally back to the TOC and told him to settle down. From then on, we assigned a soldier to watch our friend to ensure that he did not do something we would all be sorry for.

2100, 27 February-0500, 28 February 1991

At 2100, 27 February 1991, the task force received a change of mission:

"CONTINUE DOWN THE HWY 8 AXIS TO AN ATTACK POSITION. OPORD TO FOLLOW AT THE ASSAULT CP AT 272400 FEB. SEND A LIAISON OFFICER TO RECEIVE THE ORDER."

At this point, the "fog of war" again enshrouded the weary task force. Unknown to the task force, the division had issued a FRAGO that gave new map graphics (i.e., briefing charts, overlays, transparencies, etc.) revealing the way to Basra. For one reason or another, the task force never received a copy of these maps, which made the FRAGO pretty confusing. Since the order referred to maps unknown to the task force, the S3, by obtaining information over the radio, was able to provide a sketchy but readable picture of the situation until a copy of the maps could be secured.

Damn! We had run off without the map sheet, which in our case meant map/overlays, without which the order made little sense. The SCO quickly got on the radio and sorted it out enough so that we could issue a FRAGO and some quick overlays to the troops. Up to this point, we had been successful in fighting the battle using a 1:50,000 scale map, but now the task force went almost exclusively to the 1:250,000 scale maps. By this time, the task force's orders were issued over the radio by indicating a series of "way points" or grid coordinates along the axis of advance which, on receipt, we indexed into the GPS.

An enemy and friendly forces situation update for the area was also given. Basically, by providing the mission, route, enemy and friendly forces situations, and movement formation, orders were simplified and easily understood. As we grew weary, simpler orders were better for leaders and subordinates.

The division FRAGO directed the task force to send a liaison officer (LO) to receive the order at the assault CP. The problem was that the task force LO, Captain Ivan Pawlowicz, was located at the division main command post, which was still in Saudi Arabia. The only officer available to send was the communications and electronics support officer (CESO), Captain Steve Noel. He was dispatched immediately to the assault CP to get a copy of the new map overlay and receive the new order. He was instructed to meet the task force's TOC at the new attack position. The basic scheme of maneuver was sent over the FM radio.

The task force's mission was to follow the 1st Brigade, then turn north to seize the Rumaylah oil fields and guard the northern flank of the division as it continued the attack toward Basra. The attack was set for 0600, 28 February 1991, with artillery preparatory fires to begin at 0500. At 2100, 27 February, the new LO left for the assault CP, followed at 2200 by the task force's main body en route to the attack position.

The task force issued a FRAGO for the troops to conduct a tactical road march along a two-lane road running just south of Highway 8 to close rapidly into the attack position. When the task force closed on the attack position, the orders group was to assemble, the FRAGO issued, and complete preparations to execute the attack at 0600. This was to be the first time the task force orders group, to include all the subordinate commanders, was to have met since 22 February in Saudi Arabia. It never happened.

On the way to the attack position, the column received small-arms fire from several pockets of resistance that the 1st Brigade had bypassed. The enemy fire caused A/13 FA (MLRS) to slow its movement, which resulted in the column being divided in two. Adding to the confusion, the entire movement was conducted at night and the cavalrymen were bone-tired after the many hours of constant movement.

It was at this point that the long hours of training paid off, for the cavalry troops and tank company easily and rapidly dealt with the enemy forces. Because of its firepower and protection, the tank company was selected to lead the way to ensure a rapid advance. Captain Mike Foley, the tank company's commander, was engaged several times in small attacks. He quickly maneuvered his force, destroyed the enemy, reported his actions, and then continued to move on. The SCO's intent was to move as quickly as possible into the forward attack positions in order to prepare for the next morning's attack.

However, hundreds of Iraqi soldiers who had surrendered or were trying to surrender were wandering around on the dark battlefield. Since the task force had received several small-arms attacks, wandering Iraqis were a threat. As a result, the task force did not close on its attack position until 0300, 28 February, which was much later than expected. By this time, the entire task force was physically and mentally exhausted. A planned two-hour movement had actually taken over five hours. The LO briefed the command group on the new order and also stated that a cease-fire was a possibility for the next morning.

Meanwhile, the SCO quickly issued the attack order over the radio. Later, at 0430, the TOC received a message from the division that the attack was on hold, pending the announcement of a cease-fire at 0800. In the interim, the task force refueled, rearmed, and prepared to attack into the Rumaylah oil fields at 0500--if the order was given. The artillery preparatory fires began on time.

At 0530, the TOC received a message from the division announcing that a cease-fire would be in effect at 0800. In the meantime, we were to hold our position. The troopers of the task force took the news not in the elation one would normally expect but with a sense of relief and exhaustion. The 100-hour war was over. The perimeter was established and most of the troopers put their heads down for the first time in a long while.

The night from hell! I was dead tired. The SCO looked at me and I could see that he was worse off than I. The personal toll from continuous operations was starting to creep up on us. The order to move had been issued. Expecting an uneventful move, the SCO put me in control while he got some sleep. Since we expected to continue the attack the next morning, it was important for him to rest. With that, the TAC CP moved out, followed later by the TOC.

The first few hours of the road march were tense. It was dark, and all along the road we continued to pass Iraqi soldiers streaming up the road. Since we were using blackout markers, I could not see the Iraqis until they were right next to the HMMWV. My set of PVS-7s had broken, so my driver would tell us when he saw people on the side of the road. Master Sergeant Cabrerra, Sergeant First Class Torres, the fire support section NCO in charge, and I all had our weapons locked and loaded ready for any contingency. As the night progressed, my head became heavier and heavier and I drifted in and out of sleep. Every call on the radio brought me back to life. The pace was much slower than predicted and it seemed like we had been on the road forever.

The numerous contact reports by troop commanders reminded us all of the danger in the area. Small-arms fire was not fearful for attacked vehicle crew, but those in a HMMWV were more apprehensive. I was constantly pushing the troop commanders to keep moving toward the new attack positions because we still had to issue an order when we linked up with the LO. At one point, the column broke up and Captain Foley, the lead commander, asked permission to continue to move. Fortunately, I denied his request, because just a few minutes later, he was engaged by small-arms fire, which he quickly and easily dealt with.

At around 0300, the TOC closed on the TAC CP and the squadron commander assumed control. I slumped over in my seat for another short rest. Since I had made a land navigation mistake during the move, the task force was about five kilometers south of the attack position. The SCO recognized the error immediately and began reorienting the task force to the north.

Soon, the SCO and S3 linked up with Captain Noel and were debriefed. Noel informed him that the possibility of a cease-fire the next morning was high, yet the CG wanted us to be prepared to execute an attack following the 1st Brigade and then swing north into the Rumaylah oil fields, the task force's objective. From what I understand, I slept through one of the most impressive displays of artillery firepower anyone in the TOC had ever seen, as the massed artillery fired the preparatory fires for the attack that never occurred.

We re-positioned the TOC to the north at 0600 and when the formal cease-fire message arrived, we sat next to Highway 8 over 350 kilometers from TAA Quarter. In celebration of the cease-fire, I pulled a cot out of the back of my HMMWV, grabbed my United Airlines flight blanket, threw it over my head, and went to sleep.

1200, 28 February-1300, 1 March 1991

The rest was short because at 1200, 28 February 1991, the task force received another FRAGO:

"TF 2-4 CAV OPCON TO THE DISCOM. SECURE THE DIVISION SUPPORT AREA AND CONDUCT SECURITY OPERATIONS ALONG THE HIGH SPEED AVENUES OF APPROACH INTO THE DIVISION SUPPORT AREA (DSA) VICINITY JALIBAH AIRFIELD."

A FRAGO was issued to the troops, which basically placed one troop on each of three high-speed avenues of approach into the division support area. When the blocking positions were occupied and

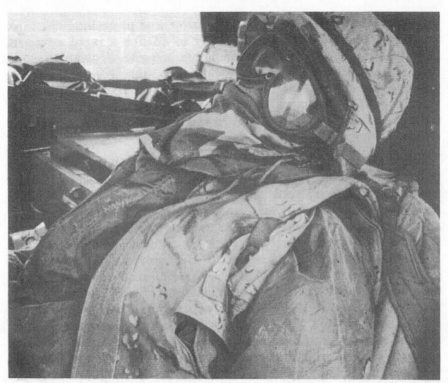

A weary trooper taking a short nap. Desert parkas, flak jackets, and goggles were standard uniform items.

the roadblocks established, the task force cleared the zone, capturing EPWs. Now in the daylight, many bypassed Iraqi positions were discovered and the Iraqis were surrendering en masse. Thus, transportation, life support, and medical care for EPWs had to be addressed.

Since the task force had no organic transportation to move the EPWs, they were marched to the nearest road and guarded until they could be collected. Meanwhile, because of the terrible condition of the EPWs, American soldiers gave them their water and MREs. As a result, a significant increase in food and water resupply operations from the combat and field trains was necessary. The field trains arrived late on the night of 28 February. Medical care was required for many of the EPWs. Fortunately, the task force was able to provide emergency medical care for the wounded Iraqis.

Additionally, refugee control, especially along Highway 8, was also a problem. At the time of the cease-fire, the division had cut

The deputy commander's HMMWV. Just before the start of the ground war, the squadron exchanged its CUCVs for HMMWVs. Unfortunately, the new vehicles had none of the basic issue items, to include the canvas and doors.

I have never seen a colder, wetter, more miserable yet ecstatic Major Lou Gelling than on the day when he finally arrived at the main command post with all the vehicles in his convoy that had been mired in the bog. It had rained for the entire 150-kilometer journey. This unsightly but proud officer reported "mission accomplished" to the commander and then collapsed from exhaustion in the TOC.

Highway 8 in the middle. Consequently, both EPWs and refugees were moving in both directions, toward Basra in the east and Baghdad in the west. The EPWs and refugees had to be separated and secured, since it was unsafe for the refugees to be moving around the area. The greatest danger was the extremely large amount of unexploded Iraqi and American ordnance strewn everywhere.

During this time, a tank platoon on Highway 8 provided security for the roadblock. The tank commander identified several trucks towing artillery pieces and a bus down the highway. A tank fired a round "over the bow" of the bus as it approached the roadblock and the concussion from the blast broke every window in the bus, causing the entire column to stop. The bus, filled with Iraqi soldiers, quickly surrendered.[19]

An MLRS battery firing a mission along Highway 8 in Iraq-an awesome sight.

The task force positioned the squadron aid station at the refugee control point, where it assisted the refugees who were traveling along Highway 8. EPW cages were also established along Highway 8. The task force established the following policy concerning refugees and EPWs: "If a man of military age is traveling with a family then consider him a refugee and do not break up the family unit. Any male of military age traveling alone or in a group was considered an EPW and transported to the EPW cage established by the MPs. All women and children were treated as refugees."[20] In fact, the task force surgeon delivered a refugee baby in the aid station in the early morning of the 28th. As in all wars, the stark images of death that surrounded the cavalry-men were mitigated by the arrival of life and the realization that life goes on.[21]

Our path back to the DSA was the same route we had traveled the night before. Only this time, it was broad daylight and the death and destruction were evident everywhere. The enemy dead were strewn all over the route, many of whom had probably been killed the night before by the same warriors who now drove past. The troopers' reactions to this grizzly scene were mixed. Some noted the weird contortions and dismemberment associated with violent death. Others just averted their eyes trying to ignore it.

Two thoughts ran through my mind: how would these dead soldiers' families ever know what had become of their loved ones, and how would I feel if these were American soldiers? Both questions were sobering. As the bodies began to bloat and stink, American soldiers began to bag, tag, and remove them from the field. Not knowing who these unfortunate American soldiers were, we all agreed that the job was not for us.

The TOC set up, and for the first time since the war began, we put up sleeping tents; we thought we would be there for a while. The S3 coordinated with the DISCOM headquarters for the security missions. We spent the rest of the day watching these huge logistics convoys descend on the DSA. After a few hours of sleep that morning, the elation and relief began to set in. That night, I sat in the now barely running HQ 30 track and wrote a letter to my family to let them know I was all right. I put it in the mail bag knowing that it would be at least several days before that mail bag went anywhere. As it turned out, I received some of these letters at my home in Hinesville, Georgia, for several months after I returned.

Next, I pulled out the TOC logs and began to reconstruct the last several days activities in my mind and in my notebook. In these notes, I concentrated on recording the facts-what happened and when. Also, over the next day, the battle captains and TOC crew were present to recall any events that were hazy and they added their own perceptions to the events.

1300-2300, 1 March 1991

At 1300, 1 March 1991, the task force received a FRAGO from division:

"MOVE TO AND ESTABLISH THE ALTERNATE PEACE NEGOTIATIONS SITE IN THE VICINITY OF THE DTAC [division tactical command post] NLT 020800 MAR 91."

Now, the division had been tasked to secure and establish a possible peace negotiations site in the vicinity of Basra. Apparently, arrangements for a peace conference were under way, and several possible sites were prepared. This particular one was not used, but the one at Safwan was.

Next, the squadron commander issued a FRAGO for A Troop to pull out of its current position and secure the peace negotiation site in the vicinity of the DTAC, located approximately thirty kilometers east of the DSA. Also, a twenty-man detail from the field trains was trucked to the site. The SCO and SXO also went to the DTAC and received further instructions from the ADC(M), Brigadier General Scott. Two CH-47s landed that evening from the division main CP with tents, tables, and chairs for the site and the troopers and an engineer platoon began establishing the negotiations site.

The SCO and I both moved to the proposed site, which was next to the DTAC. En route, I dropped off the Stars and Stripes reporter and the division's historian, Major Thomas, who had joined us just before crossing the initial line of departure. They both pitched right in and, by the end of their time with us, were accepted members of the crew. Major Thomas, a reservist, was a lawyer from Columbia, South Carolina.

The Stars and Stripes reporter requested to join the cavalry for two reasons: our unit was the first to go into Iraq, and the air cavalry troops could fly his stories to the rear for filing. He got what he wanted in the first case, but we never got a story out for him. Every once in a while, he would mention it to me during the attack and I would express my sympathy, but without fail, within the hour, we would hear those two words that brought groans from the TOC crew, "Jump it."

The reporter wore civilian clothes and rode as one of the five or six people in the HQ 30 at any one time. It was not until I was driving him to the assault command post to drop him off that I discovered he was an Active Army Sergeant. He certainly did not act or look like one.

On the afternoon of 1 March, we walked the site and directed the engineers and our soldiers in preparing the site and erecting tents and other paraphernalia. At dusk, the SCO attended a commander's meeting at the assault command post. I remained in charge at the peace negotiations site and spent another night in the front seat of my HMMWV.

Enemy prisoners of war. Besides their age and semblance of a military uniform, it was often difficult to tell the soldiers from the refugees. Massive EPW operations can stop offensive operations cold.

After our fiasco of not having the correct maps and graphics on the night preceding the cease-fire, the S2 and S3 ensured that we had the proper 1:50,000 maps and the correct division graphics in case of any further combat operations. The graphics were easy to obtain; the maps were not because the division's basic load of maps had been left in Saudi Arabia. Fortunately, the division main command post was ordered to move north into Iraq that day. As is normal practice, a skeleton battle staff was flown to the DTAC while the main CP was moving. Our S2 had provided the G2 with a list of maps that we needed and the next morning, Captain Elizabeth Schwab, from the division G2 section, presented me with several plastic bags full of the needed maps.

The **peace negotiations site** in the vicinity of Jalibah Airfield. In the foreground is a burned-out Iraqi PT-76 used as window dressing. In the background is the ten-foot berm constructed around the actual site, which consisted of several large military tents.

2300, 1 March-0600, 2 March 1991

At 2300, 1 March 1991, the task force received a FRAGO from division:

"CONTINUE TO PREPARE THE PEACE NEGOTIATIONS SITE. CONDUCT A FORWARD PASSAGE OF LINES AT 020600 MAR 91 THROUGH THE 1ST BDE TO REESTABLISH THE DIVISION'S SECURITY ZONE."

The SCO personally received this mission from the commanding general at the commanders meeting at the assault command post. At this meeting, the division commander directed the division to halt its forward movement but not to give up any ground or to take any risks. He instructed the commanders to defend themselves vigorously if attacked.

After the meeting, the SCO talked to the commanding general and proposed that the task force reestablish the security zone in front of the division and screen the division, which would allow the brigades to reconstitute. The commanding general agreed and instructed the SCO to move out at dawn the next day and establish a ten-kilometer security zone in front of the division. The SCO and the 1st Brigade's commander coordinated the passage and Colonel John LeMoyne said he would send his scout platoons out to the limit of

-100-

advance (PL Crush) that night in preparation for the arrival of TF 2-4 Cav.[22]

The SCO returned to the TOC where he issued the FRAGO to move forward, pass through the 1st Brigade, and reestablish the security zone out to PL Crush. Meanwhile, the SXO continued to prepare the peace negotiations site until 0630. He then linked up with the TOC along Highway 8 behind the lead troops and collocated with the 1st Brigade's TAC CP. The SXO issued the maps to the troop TOCs or commanders as they passed along Highway 8.

The task force was to maintain two sets of 1:50,000 and 1:250,000 maps. Most orders and plans were issued in 1:250,000 scale, but the task force had fought off 1:50,000 scale maps. The translation of map overlays and map scales was always a challenge to the entire chain of command. However, the use of global positioning systems and combat reconnaissance patrols ahead of the lead troops made establishing checkpoints easy, which added to the high mobility of the task force throughout the attack.

After the SCO completed the meeting at the assault command post, he informed me of the new missions. He instructed me to remain at the peace negotiations site with A Troop and the detail from HHT. The SCO was en route to the TOC, where he and the S3 would get the remainder of the task force moving east to hit the passage points with 1st Brigade at first light. The peace negotiations site was near the 1st Brigade's TAC CP where our TOC would collocate during the passage. My plan was to link up with them there.

0600-1600, 2 March 1991

The task force had moved forward, coordinated with the 1st Brigade, and was beginning the forward passage of the 1st Brigade when the 1st Brigade scouts reported contact with a large enemy armored formation (see Map 13). A battle at the Rumaylah oil fields ensued. The task force was ordered to stop behind the 1st Brigade along Highway 8 and act as the division reserve until the fight was completed or the task force was committed.

The battle at the Rumaylah oil fields raged as the task force waited to move forward. At 0900, the squadron moved forward to reestablish the security zone. Since the 1st Brigade had made enemy contact, the task force's sector was shifted to the south and the security zone established in front of the 2d Brigade. During this period, the squadron destroyed several air defense artillery sites, tracked and wheeled vehicles, and various supply and ammunition storage points.

I was standing in the middle of Highway 8 madly issuing maps to the troops when the task force was ordered to stop. Since I had missed the earlier artillery barrage just before the cease-fire, I was startled when an MLRS battalion fired what seemed to be a full volley about 1,000 meters to my right or south-an impressive display to say the least.

1600-1900, 2 March 1991

At 1600, 2 March 1991, the task force received a FRAGO from division:

"REESTABLISH THE SECURITY ZONE IN FRONT OF THE 2D BRIGADE IN THE SOUTH DIVISION SECTOR. ESTABLISH CONTACT WITH 3 ACR ON DIVISION SOUTHERN FLANK AND SECURE AREA BETWEEN 24 ID(M) AND 3 ACR."

The task force now moved forward with three troops of cavalry abreast oriented on the high-speed avenues of approach. A Troop was in the north, D/3-69 Armor in the center, and D/4 Cav in the south. The task force TOC established contact with 3 ACR via FM radio, and the SCO personally effected coordination with it on the southern flank as the task force closed into position. On completion of the operation, the task force established and secured the division's limit of advance,which was PL Crush.

When I finally rejoined the TOC, I discovered that the HQ 30 had finally died. Master Sergeant Cabrerra had cross-loaded equipment and supplies as best he could and we were now operating out of the S2's, fire support officer's, and engineer's M577s. In the cross-loading procedure, we had forgotten one very important item, the Communications-Electronics Operation Instructions (CEOI), which remained on the HQ 30. As so often happens, the first time we really needed to make contact with 3 ACR, we did not have the necessary instructions. After some embarrassment, however, we obtained the correct frequencies and call signs required to establish contact. Luckily,we were near the end of our journey and the HQ 30 would catch up the next

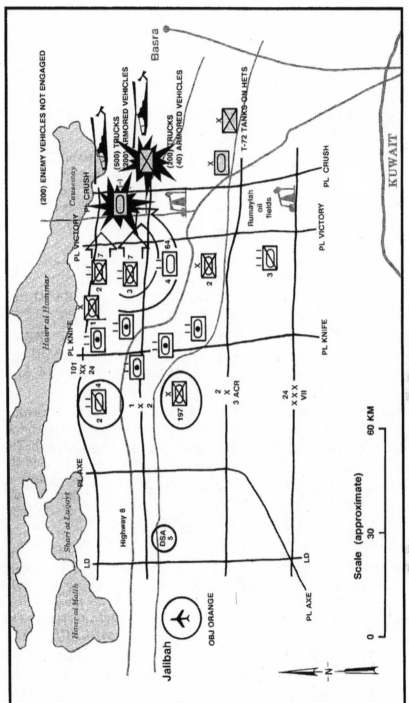

Map 13. Battle of Rumaylah

-103-

day. But a high-speed drive of over 100 kilometers was still required to secure this very important document.

When the TOC was established and the task force's sector occupied, the command group focused on consolidating the task force. Major Gelling and Command Sergeant Major Soucy were both dispatched back along the route of march to bring forward all the stranded vehicles. Major Gelling was to return to the bog and secure the forces left there. Because of the limited range of the FM radios, the multiple reorganizations of the task force, and vehicle breakdowns, it took twenty-four hours to account for every trooper in the task force.

1900, 2 March-6 March 1991

For the next several days, the task force blocked the roads leading into its sector and continued separating the refugees from the EPWs. The only difference now was that the EPWs were not controlled by U.S. forces; they were instructed to return to the east and the Iraqi side of the demilitarized zone (DMZ).

Additionally, the task force began the systematic destruction of all Iraqi military equipment and stores in the sector. In fact, in the center of the task force sector was an ammunition dump with at least 500 ammunition bunkers, of which less than 5 had been destroyed on arrival. The relatively undamaged condition of this huge, clearly marked target sheds some light on the actual destruction caused by the aerial campaign. In this ammunition storage depot, cavalry scouts and combat engineers from A/3 Engr spent almost five days conducting demolition operations. Unfortunately, the task force's only serious casualties were sustained at this ammunition storage site, when a first lieutenant and a sergeant from A/3 Engr were injured and evacuated.

During this period, I made daily rounds to the troops. While visiting D/3-69 Armor, I heard and felt a tremendous explosion coming from the direction of the ammunition dump. Within the next minute, I heard the call for MEDEVAC (medical evacuation) on the command radio net. I quickly moved to the ammunition dump. When I arrived, the lieutenant and sergeant had already been transported to the aerial MEDEVAC pickup site at the edge of the ammunition dump. The lieutenant was on the hood of a HMMWV bleeding profusely from the ears and nose and being attended to by a medic.

The sergeant was sitting on a stretcher next to the HMMWV drinking water. The sergeant was badly burned. The MEDEVAC helicopter arrived within ten minutes of the initial call and the two wounded soldiers were evacuated. Both recovered but were never returned to the unit while in country.

Many times during the dash to the river valley, the task force did not detain Iraqi soldiers. These **Iraqi soldiers** were disarmed, stripped of any military equipment besides their personal kit, given several MREs, pointed in the right direction, and told to go home.

At the direction of the SCO, I immediately began investigating the cause of the accident. After looking at the accident site and interviewing the witnesses, I concluded that a combination of poor judgment, overwork, and other circumstances caused the two injuries. The platoon had been destroying bunkers for several days. The incident occurred late in the afternoon. The platoon had run out of detonation primers and had begun using Iraqi grenade primers. Since the bunker contained more ammunition than expected and a quicker fuse burn time, a much faster and larger explosion occurred than expected. Consequently, the lieutenant and sergeant's HMMWV was caught in the blast. The rear of the HMMWV was completely blown away and the vehicle lay only a few meters from the crater. It was a miracle the men inside survived.

The squadron commander with the press. This crew televised the last large ammunition complex to be destroyed by the division.

On 4 March 1991, the DCO, Major Gelling, arrived at the TOC leading a convoy of all the vehicles that had been mired in the bog, and the squadron maintenance officer (SMO) had collected all the vehicles from the various unit maintenance collection points. This recovery operation was truly a herculean effort by all the soldiers involved, especially Captain Jeff Kelley, the SMO, and Chief Warrant Officer Curlen Richardson, the squadron maintenance technician.

The task force was now completely intact for the first time since leaving TAA Saber on 23 February 1991.[23]

2200, 4 March 1991

The following FRAGO was received from division:

"PREPARE 30 SOLDIERS FROM THE SQUADRON FOR REDE-PLOYMENT. REPORT TO JALIBAH AIR FIELD BY 050900 MAR 91 FOR REDEPLOYMENT BACK TO FORT STEWART."

The end was near! Thirty troopers were assembled at the task force TOC under the control of the task force S3 and then escorted by

Blast from the Iraqi ammunition depot. This picture was taken from the vicinity of the main command post, which was approximately five kilometers from the depot. The bunker complex was huge and explosions of this size were common. Unfortunately, it was one of these types of explosions that wounded the two soldiers from A/3 Engr assigned to the task force. For the most part, the engineers and cavalry scouts had no idea how the huge ammunition stockpiles would react when detonated. It was almost impossible to predict the size of the secondary explosions.

the command sergeant major to Jalibah Airfield. These troopers were selected by their chain of command. The commander's guidance was to pick troopers who could conduct quartering operations at Fort Stewart and await for the arrival of the main body. The SCO stressed to the leaders that this was not a reward but another important mission. Since there was no squadron rear detachment, no one knew what they would find at Fort Stewart.

The rumors were rampant. In fact, the squadron returned to an entirely new set of billets and motor pool. Several days later, they were the first Victory Division soldiers to return to Fort Stewart. The remainder of the task force continued the mission. The cavalry men's work was not yet done.

The squadron S3, Captain Pete Utley, was selected by the SCO to lead the cavalry contingent home. He and four other members of the TOC crew packed their bags, said their quick good-byes, and left the next morning. Captain Rans Black assumed the duties as the S3 operations officer.

On 6 March 1991, the task force was ordered by the division to conduct reconnaissance along three routes from its current locations along the DMZ through Kuwait to a proposed division marshaling area just north of Kuwait City. This marshaling area would be used to stage the division's movement back to the port of Dammam, Saudi Arabia, for redeployment to the United States. The route to the marshaling area used the best roads along the most direct route to Dammam. The other option was to return basically along the same routes on which the task force had attacked.

The division attached TF Air Cav, consisting of the two air cavalry troops, to the task force to assist in the reconnaissance mission. Each troop was given one route to reconnoiter--D/3-69 Armoron the left, A Troop in the center, and D/4 Cav on the right. Meanwhile, the air cavalry conducted reconnaissance ahead of the troops along all three routes. The SCO and SXO also moved along these routes in UH-60 helicopters to command and control the operation and verify the routes.

On arrival in the proposed marshaling area, the SXO linked up with elements of the British 1st Armored Division and the ADC(S), Brigadier General Frazar, and coordinated the division's movement plan. The initial reconnaissance was executed in HMMWVs, with the exception of the center route, which was executed by all of A Troop. The task force's TAC CP accompanied A Troop and when the SCO arrived by UH-60, he stayed on the ground in the TAC CP as the forward command and control element while the SXO returned to the TOC.

A Troop was to secure the marshaling area, while the remainder of the task force returned to its original positions the next day (7 March). On 8 March, the TOC received the message that the redeployment through Kuwait had been disapproved and that the task force was to return to its sector and prepare for future operations.

The change in the mission-canceling the redeployment through Kuwait and directing us back along our old attack route-was a blow to task force morale. Under the reorientation, the task force also went from being the lead element of the division to being the trailing unit.

During the reconnaissance into Kuwait, the task force lost its Kuwaiti interpreter and friend, Wally. He accompanied the SCO and the TAC CP on the reconnaissance with glee because he knew he was moving toward home. In fact, the assembly area in Kuwait where A Troop and the TAC CP spent the night was within thirty kilometers of Kuwait City. Upon learning late in the afternoon that the task force was being recalled into Iraq, Wally decided to go home. He went out on the highway and made his way to his house. Early the next morning, he reappeared at the TAC CP and reported that his family was fine but that the living conditions in Kuwait City were terrible. The TAC crew gave him some bottled water and MREs and sent him on his way. It was an emotional good-bye. [24]

At 1500, 8 March 1991, while withdrawing from the marshaling area in Kuwait, TF Air Cav discovered an airfield and built-up area in the center portion of the sector. The air cavalry reported several hundred Iraqi soldiers and numerous armored vehicles and trucks occupying the airfield. The task force was brought to REDCON 1 and an AH-64 company was put under its operational control to assist as the situation developed.

Additionally, the division sent a psychological operations (PSYOP) team aboard a UH-1 to assist. The UH-1 landed at the task force TOG where twenty cases of MREs were loaded on board for possible distribution to the Iraqi soldiers. Then, elements of the task force moved out and quickly established overwatch positions at the airfield. The PSYOP team landed and spoke by loudspeaker to the Iraqi soldiers, informing them that the war was over and to begin moving to the northeast to clear the U.S. zone. After discussions with the Iraqi leadership, it was decided that the Iraqis would begin moving at first light the next morning. The Iraqi soldiers were smart not to begin their movement at night, for the desert was dangerous at night, especially for dismounted troops. On 9 March, the task force swept the area and used organic transportation and several Iraqi trucks to escort the Iraqis back across the DMZ.

Further interrogation of the Iraqi prisoners revealed that the walled compound was a conference center used primarily by the Iraqi defense minister. On 9 March, the Iraqi soldiers were evacuated, and the complex and all the military vehicles and equipment around it were destroyed.

During the conduct of these reconnaissance operations, the roadblocks were still occupied along the high-speed avenues of approach into the division sector. The troopers manning these roadblocks were constantly having to sort out the Iraqi soldiers and the refugees. The Iraqi soldiers were turned back and the refugees were allowed to pass. The troopers sent everyone they were not sure of to the TOC to be sorted out. I'll recount two cases.

The first concerned an Iraqi national who had been educated at the University of Pittsburgh and was married to an American. Before the war, he had returned to Iraq to teach and had brought his family. After the war began, he and his family had tried to return to the United States. The family, being American citizens, had been allowed to leave, but he was denied. Therefore, he returned to work at the University of Basra. According to him, after the cease-fire, the conditions in Basra were incredible-including open fighting in the streets between the Iraqi Army, police, and rebels. That day, he packed a suitcase, got in his car, and drove west, fearing for his life. Upon being stopped at the roadblock, he got out of his car and turned himself over to the nearest American soldier and pleaded his case. He was transported to the TOC, where I spoke to him. He spoke perfect English, had pictures of his family, and a Pennsylvania driver's license. What finally convinced me that he was not the enemy was when he produced a Zayre's credit card. He was turned over to the division G5 at the main command post and subsequently evacuated through refugee channels to Saudi Arabia.

The second incident involved an Iraqi officer whose rank was equivalent to our captain. His story, as translated through a military interpreter, went something like this. He could not return to Kuwait because the civilian population believed he was a war criminal and would kill him. He could not return to the Iraqi Army because what he really was doing was assisting the Kuwaiti underground resistance movement against the Iraqis. If the Iraqi Army found him, he would be killed. Therefore, the only place he would be safe was in America, and he was requesting some form of political asylum. After thinking about this one for about two seconds, I had this gentleman packed up and returned to the roadblock with the instructions that he not be allowed on the U.S. side of the DMZ.

9 March 1991

This FRAGO was received from division:

"CONDUCT REAR GUARD OPERATIONS FOR THE DIVISION AS IT RETIRES FROM IRAQ."

Elements of the 1st Cavalry Division relieved the task force in place and it was now reorganized for a new mission. The new task organization added a mechanized infantry company from 3-15 Inf and a 155-mm howitzer battery from the 3-41 FA to replace the MLRS battery. A large maintenance detachment from C Company, 724th Main Support Battalion, with twenty HETs was also attached to recover stranded vehicles along the march route. Additionally, the task force retained control of the air cavalry troops.

On 8 March, a tank-heavy task force of the 1st Cavalry Division occupied an assembly area next to the TOC. That afternoon, I went to its TOC to coordinate for the relief in place. As I walked into the TOC, the first question they asked me was, "Is there an NBC threat in the area?" This question puzzled me since there was no threat nor had there been. Then it dawned on me that I was still wearing my MOPP suit and flak vest, which had been the standard gear in the 24th Division since 16 January. They were wearing only their combat vehicle coverall uniforms. I longed for the day when I could take the nasty MOPP suit off, but I wore it as a badge of honor among these soldiers from another division.

While preparing to move, the task force received an order to distribute MREs to the local populace and refugees. Thereafter, several trailer loads of MREs were delivered to grateful Iraqi people. In fact, the Iraqis were so zealous at times that troopers had to form a cordon to keep the children from being crushed as the pallets of MREs were dumped off the trucks.

On 11 March, the commanding general visited the TOC and spoke to the command and staff group, reporting that the task force had "covered itself with glory." The magnitude of the task force's accomplishments had still not dawned on the majority of the soldiers. The news from outside the division was scarce, and all we really knew was that we had won "big."

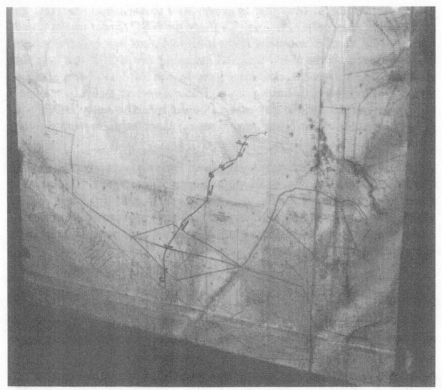

A main command post map. The map marks the road march route out of Iraq. The map is a1:250,000-scale map, which was used in conjunction with the 1:50,000-scale maps. Transposing data from one map scale to another was a challenge. This process usually resulted in significantly degraded accuracy of the graphics.

The division's graphics were published on a 1:250,000-scale map, but the task force fought off the 1:50,000-scale map. The maps still had the neutral zone between Saudi Arabia and Iraq marked. Since this political boundary had little meaning, the boundary actually split the difference. The boundary itself was not physically marked on the ground except by a series of berms. These berms did not follow any azimuth and were often just mounds of dirt.

On 12 March, after destroying another large ammunition storage area in one huge explosion, the task force began its last mission in Iraq, which was to be the division's rear guard. Thankfully, the rear guard mission was relatively uneventful. The air cavalry troops swept a twenty-kilometer-wide swath of the desert along the route, ensuring that no vehicles had wandered away and become stranded. The HETs were busy recovering vehicles along the route under control of the

DCO. The first day, the task force moved to a refueling site located at the half-way point and formed a laager for the night. On the morning of 13 March, the task force followed the assault command post down the route out of Iraq and back into Saudi Arabia.

The refueling site was like a huge gas station in the middle of the desert. At dusk, the task force began refueling. We were instructed to stop at the far side of the refueling site and pick up our food for the rest of the journey. Since we had eaten nothing but MREs since before the attack, we expected to be thrown a couple more MREs and sent on our way. Amazingly, as we approached vehicles parked on the side of the trail, a soldier ran out and asked how many people were in the vehicle. We were then given a burlap bag for each soldier and directed to move on.

Inside the burlap bag was a feast of cookies, candy, soda, and individual servings of canned stew, lasagna, or other delectables (pogey bait!). Food from the local McDonald's will never taste as good as the food in those burlap bags tasted that night.

We occupied a tactical assembly area that night close to the refueling site. The next morning, the assault command post, with the commanding general aboard his Bradley fighting vehicle, hit the start point, and we followed close behind.

At 0100, 14 March 1991, the squadron commander stood at the border and watched as the last elements of the task force crossed into Saudi Arabia. The SCO, as he crossed into Saudi Arabia, was the last 24 ID(M) soldier out of Iraq. The task force was first into Iraq and last out-one hell of a ride. The SCO reported to the commanding general that the 24th Infantry Division was clear of Iraq. The task force was then reorganized and all the attachments were returned to their parent units. The squadron began redeployment operations through the port of Dammam, back to Fort Stewart, and then home.

At 1000, 14 March, the squadron completed its last mission when the squadron assembled at the field trains to "thank God" that all the troopers of the squadron had accomplished their mission with no deaths or serious injuries. Chaplain Dan Payne delivered a moving sermon, and again, all the "troopers stood by their mounts."

Cavalry chaplain, Captain Dan Payne, whose performance was superb. In peace time, the chaplain's need for a vehicle is often questioned, but the troopers of the task force were happy when he unexpectedly arrived in their area.

IX. OPERATIONAL SUMMARY

From 23 February to 12 March 1991, elements of TF 2-4 Cav conducted various combat missions over 370 kilometers of enemy territory from the Saudi Arabian-Iraqi border to within 40 kilometers due west of Basra, Iraq. During this period, the task force conducted virtually every cavalry operation under the control of every maneuver brigade in the division and the division support command. The task force protected the division as it moved into the forward attack position, led the division main effort into Iraq, protected the flank of the division, and became the division reserve. It performed route and zone reconnaissance and, as both a screening and guard force, conducted advanced, flank, and rear security operations (see Map 14).

The task force came in contact with elements of the 26th Commando Brigade, the 47th and 49th Infantry Divisions, and four Republican Guards divisions. It captured in excess of 1,000 EPWs and destroyed a large amount of equipment and materiel (as shown in Table 5). These totals represent approximately a mechanized brigade's worth of organic assets, including supporting artillery, air defense, and support vehicles. Numerous caches of small arms and ammunition were also destroyed. Also destroyed were two major ammunition depots containing an estimated 80,000 rounds of 100-mm or greater tank and artillery rounds.[25] A Company, 3d Engineers, and cavalry scouts spent eight days conducting bunker-to-bunker destruction of the ammunition dumps. Few of the Iraqi vehicles had been destroyed in close combat; most had been abandoned.

The task force engaged in two significant actions. Friendly losses were minimal. No one in the task force was killed in action. Several soldiers with minor shrapnel injuries were treated at the task force aid station and then quickly returned to duty. Two men wounded in action required aerial medical evacuation.

Overall, it was quite a ride. The troopers of TF 2-4 Cav were deployed to Southwest Asia for seven months. The result was no surprise. It just demonstrated once again that the American soldier is the best in the world and that American junior officers and NCOs are truly superb. The generals won this war at the operational level with a great plan. The success of the generals and their skill in the operational art kept the soldiers, like the troopers of TF 2-4 Cav, from having to win this war in the trenches, wadis, and sepkas with their blood.

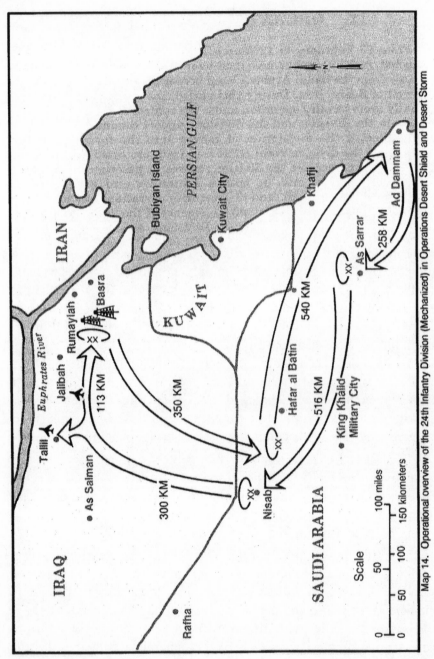

Map 14. Operational overview of the 24th Infantry Division (Mechanized) in Operations Desert Shield and Desert Storm

Table 5. Equipment and Materiel Destroyed by TF 2-4 Cav

Equipment	Number Destroyed
T-72M1	21
T-62	4
T-55	25
PT-76	2
TYPE 69 TANK	1
BMP1	68
MTLB	29
BRDM	16
2S3(HOW)	6
TOWED ARTILLERY PIECES	30
ZPU-1/2/3	27
S-60	9
ZSU 23-4	1
SA-13	1
2 1/2-TON TRUCKS	121
MISCELLANEOUS TRUCKS	342
DUMP TRUCKS	5
HETs	13
JEEPS	69
BULLDOZERS	3
MISCELLANEOUS TRAILERS	109

Major General Barry R. McCaffrey stated: "[The] legacy is two million free Kuwaiti citizens and an enduring message to both free and oppressed people throughout the world. ... There is hope; freedom is never without cost, and Americans will fight and die for our principles."[26]

X. CONCLUSIONS

TF 2-4 Cav spent five months deploying and preparing to fight, four weeks conducting combat operations in the covering-force area, and four days attacking into Iraq. The mission was accomplished, and the troopers came home and basked in the glow of a grateful nation's praise. Certainly, this work is not the detached examination of a long-past historical event by a wizened scholar. Rather, it is a record of the events and emotions experienced by a professional soldier who participated in a great event.

The professional challenge now is to draw the correct lessons from this war and prepare our Army for future operations in support of the president's national security strategy. TF2-4 Cav's example is different, remarkable, and instructive because of its level of training, organization, and leadership situation. The task force's application of Air Land Battle doctrine and its will to succeed were also instrumental elements in its success and offer useful lessons.

Training

The squadron's primary role prior to August 1990, as the 24th Motorized Rifle Battalion, was to act as the opposing force during training exercises at Fort Stewart. Basically, the task force helped prepare the division's other maneuver task forces for their National Training Center rotations. This focus on short-term training exercises, however, significantly degraded the squadron's level of training. It was believed that an aggressive precombat training program could quickly bring the squadron up to the training standard if the situation warranted. The urgency of the deployment to the Persian Gulf, however, did not allow enough time to conduct pre-deployment training for the task force.

The training program during Operation Desert Shield demon-strates that the task force's precombat training, while aggressive, was focused at the lowest unit levels. This occurred because collective training at the troop or squadron level is expensive to conduct. More-over, readiness means having fully operational vehicles, bountiful resupply assets, and fresh leaders and soldiers. High-value maneuver training creates broken vehicles, uses fuel and ammunition, and causes injuries, which all degrade combat readiness. Therefore, even though the task force did not fight for five months prior to Operation Desert Storm, neither did it execute a training program involving large formations. In fact, the only effective training took place when the task force rehearsed its operations just before crossing into Iraq. Commanders must consider the training versus readiness paradox. In order to ensure that units are properly prepared for combat, leaders must understand that training and readiness operate against each other, and this must be strictly controlled.

Recreation activities were critical during combat in the desert. To maintain high morale,leaders created opportunities for soldiers to relax and unwind.

The task force overcame this shortfall in training because its leadership recognized the problem immediately and was not lulled into a false sense of security. Throughout the deployment, the task force operated with from three to six company-size maneuver elements. Prior to deployment, the squadron had only one organic subordinate maneuver troop; A Troop.

The second organic ground troop was designed to come from the 3d Brigade's separate cavalry troop (either an Active or Reserve Component unit). Multi-echeloned training with the air cavalry troops was limited at best. Consequently, the task force's leadership never believed that its units had trained according to its standing operating procedures, that the task force was a cohesive whole, or that the task force was blessed with the high esprit de corps normally associated with units that have commonly trained as a combined arms task force. Understanding the situation, the task force's leaders confronted the challenge and aggressively pursued training programs in Saudi Arabia. While the task force succeeded in spite of adversity, institutional corrections will prevent similar situations from happening in the future.

The Army has prided itself on its realistic training. The Army performed better in Operation Desert Storm than it did in training exercises, but it did not always appear that way. Two examples attest to this. On the one hand, soldiers often acted in highly disciplined ways. Just before crossing into Iraq, the task force opened small-arms ranges to test-fire weapons. I gave the mission of finding and running the range to one of the NCOs from the TOC.

After an hour or so, I heard rounds being fired, so I wandered down to the range to observe the training and to test-fire my weapons. First, I was intercepted by a guard who directed me to the briefing area where an NCO put me in a firing order and gave the safety briefing. Then, my weapons were inspected for proper functioning and cleanliness and I acted as an assistant instructor for the soldier who was to fire before me. I subsequently test-fired my M-16A2 rifle and M-9 pistol, was cleared from the range, and was directed to another NCO who had cleaning materials on hand and was supervising weapons maintenance.

These examples reveal professional soldiers who knew their business. We must capture this professionalism as a part of our Army's culture forever. So do we train as we fight? No-we fight better than we train because the entire unit is focused on combat-winning with the fewest casualties possible. Soldiers understand combat but do not understand some of our peacetime training quirks. Just because we were in the desert in an actual war zone did not mean we were constantly training as we would have in peacetime.

Certainly, no one disturbed a sleeping soldier unless it was absolutely necessary. It was common to see a soldier in his physical training uniform sitting in the shade eating a bag of candy or cookies, wearing a pair of tinted sunglasses and cassette player earphones on his head, and writing a letter or reading a book. Not once did I see that soldier chastised for being out of uniform or breaking a rule that is applied in many units during peacetime. Rest assured, when that soldier was called to perform, he did so magnificently.

Sometimes, the task force received equipment without knowing quite what to do with it. Shortly before crossing into Iraq, this large **psychological operations loudspeaker system** was issued to the task force. Mounted on a HMMWV, it played "inspirational and motivational" rock and roll throughout the operation.

Personally, I crossed the berm into Iraq with Jimmy Buffet playing full blast on my $10 sand-filled Radio Shack tape player, and I assure you, I was paying close attention to the matter at hand. Soldiers deal with stress in a variety of ways, a few of which are dysfunctional. Unless taken to the extreme, rarely do they indicate poor discipline.

Organization

The mechanized division commander's "eyes and ears," his "household cavalry," is the divisional cavalry squadron. This is not an assertion but a statement of fact among the senior mechanized warriors of the Army. This realization should be institutionally accepted and acted upon in equipping and organizing our mechanized and armored divisional cavalry in peacetime to prepare it for war.

First, there must be only one type of cavalry troop in the Army and it must include tanks. The "common" cavalry troop should be modeled after the current regimental cavalry troop, which has four platoons--two scout and two tank. Every divisional squadron must have three of these common troops as opposed to the two in the current configuration. All of the U.S. Army's tactical techniques and procedures are modeled around three or four sub-units. Therefore, the new divisional squadron will meet these parameters by having three four-platoon troops. The organic tank and cavalry fighting vehicle mix under the four-platoon and three-troop squadrons perfectly fulfills the division commander's requirements--all the time and under all conditions.

Second, given a robust common cavalry troop, the air cavalry assets are not mission essential to the success of the unit. The task force learned never to count on aviation assets (to include the air cavalry) for the accomplishment of critical tasks. Sometimes, weather conditions just will not permit air assets to move. For instance, because of either illumination or the weather, no combat helicopter operations were conducted for over 40 of the 100 hours of Operation Desert Storm. Even though air assets are tremendous combat multipliers, they cannot maintain operations for twenty-four hours a day and in all weather conditions. This applies especially to the divisional cavalry squadron with its current AH-1F and OH-58C helicopters.

In the armored cavalry regiments, the aviation assets are all located under a separate squadron at the regimental level. In the division, they should remain a divisional asset under the aviation brigade. Therefore, the divisional cavalry squadron should be a separate divisional battalion, not a part of the aviation brigade, as it is now. If the Army is serious about training as it fights, then the squadron's proper alignment is as a divisional asset. If it fights separately, then it should train separately.

Leadership

Fortunately, the mystical yet powerful bonding of warriors in adversity created virtually immediate cohesion throughout the task force simply through the turn of events. TF 2-4 Cav was the first mechanized unit deployed into the desert and it lived there for almost four weeks. In a theater so underdeveloped, nothing was easy and the task force lived through every challenge imaginable except open combat. Thus, it became stronger. Food, water, mail, fuel, repair parts, and basic soldier-comfort items were difficult to obtain.

Being immediately deployed deep into the desert, a long way

from anywhere in a situation where the transportation network was rudimentary at best, caused things ordinarily taken for granted to become herculean tasks. Therefore, with every passing day, the troopers of the task force gained pride, esprit, and cohesiveness because they became more and more "desert tough." Every trooper stood a little stronger and taller when he stated, "I'm in the CAV!"

The task force's change of command in January and the subsequent challenge faced by the new squadron commander is a fascinating case study in leadership. As military analysts sort through all of the organizational, personal, and cohesion issues from Operation Desert Storm, they will find some fascinating vignettes to study. Lieutenant Colonel Leney was a successful leader for several reasons. First, he personally visited each platoon-size element in the task force within fourteen days after assuming command. Personal contact is critical to unit cohesion. Second, he allowed his new staff to plan and execute the R&S mission while he concentrated on visiting each platoon during those critical first few days. Fortunately, his policy paid off and he spent valuable time with every platoon in the squadron.

Since the task force was already executing the security mission, it would have been easier for the new commander to stay at the TOC controlling the operations and supervising the planning. However, Leney provided guidance and then allowed his staff members to accomplish their tasks. Third, he led the task force from the front, even though he was often out of direct communications with higher headquarters. The command group was always with the lead troop observing events as they happened, and there is no substitute for personal observation.

The final factor, which does not relate directly to but certainly played a part in the task force's success, was that the troop- and company-level leadership did not significantly change while alterations occurred at the task force level. Thus, troop- and company-level commanders were allowed to concentrate on their missions and integrate task force changes more routinely.

AirLand Battle Doctrine

As stated previously, the skill of the senior leaders in the theater created the conditions at the operational level for such grand success, with so few casualties at the tactical level. At the same time, AirLand Battle Doctrine provided a base of knowledge and understanding for all leaders to understand the commander's intent. This is a credit to the formal schooling system of the Army. A task force executive officer could look at the map and hear or read a concept and understand the CENTCOM commander in chief's intent because of an understanding of the battlefield framework, center of gravity, and other concepts of the operational art from training at the Command and General Staff College. Also, a clear understanding of the intent of higher commanders in the command chain translates into coherent tactical goals.

Even though there are many interpretations of AirLand Battle Doctrine, its framework gives a common basis for communication leading to mutual understanding. This incredible strength of the institution must continue to be developed and nurtured, for it allows us the proper framework for meaningful dialogue focused on overwhelming victory on any battlefield.

U.S. doctrine worked in this mid-intensity conflict. In fact, the American armed forces were so successful that they have ensured the unlikelihood of other military forces challenging the United States in open warfare at the mid-intensity level. Some say that the next time we will not be so lucky in having an enemy wait six months for us to build our strength and that rapid strategic deployability should be our focus. These naysayers have little faith in the force of the American will and the ingenuity and professional competence of the American armed forces.

The U.S. armed forces simply played the cards they were dealt. But make no mistake, the goal was clear, and even if Saddam had continued the attack in August 1990, the result would have been the same, only the details would have been different. The campaign maps may have included the whole of the Saudi Arabian peninsula and four days might have been transformed into four months, but the end would have remained the same. Therefore, the new warfighting documents should review the new face of the most dangerous and most likely conflicts, learn from the Southwest Asian campaign, and focus on operations other than war as our next significant intellectual challenge while maintaining a sharp focus on warfighting.

Logistics

No discussion of this campaign would be complete without recognizing the tremendous success of the thousands of logisticians who made sure that TF 2-4 Cav and hundreds of other task forces had the means to accomplish their objectives. The in-theater logistician was forced to accomplish incredible operational missions. The Army tasked logisticians to sustain mid-intensity, mechanized combat operations in an undeveloped theater halfway around the world. Two mechanized corps were moved to positions from 250 to 500 kilometers from their nearest logistical base. And yet logisticians were expected to support them along two two-lane roads with no access to railroads. Without citing a long litany of accomplishments by these wild-eyed and crazed logisticians, it is sufficient to say that the success of TF 2-4 Cav was as much due to the truck driver as to the cavalry scout.

American Will

The support of the American people and the depth of the American will was a tremendous combat multiplier. The American soldier felt good about what he was doing. We really had no idea how demonstrative the American support was until we returned home. Certainly, the national leaders of the country ensured that the strategy was sound and they mobilized the country to the call. After establishing the strategic goals, they stuck by them no matter how unpopular and allowed military professionals to execute the strategy.

Further strengthening the American cause were the young men and women of the armed forces. The sons, daughters, sisters, brothers, husbands, and wives who served were a direct reflection of the quality and will of the American people. While the Army has its fair share of problems, the soldiers I observed possessed a moral fiber, compassion, discipline, and dedication that inspired me daily and were a direct reflection of the society we all serve.

Morality in war is difficult. One day all the rules of normal society are firmly in place; the next day, in a war setting, the rules are quite different; and then, the rules are all in place again. It requires exceptional judgment and maturity by soldiers to deal with these sorts of situations and nearly all met the challenge.

Finally, the American ethic of hard work, ingenuity, and pride daily overcame adversity. At a time when the quality of the American citizen is being compared daily to the Japanese and other foreign workers and societies, no one can question the magnitude of our accomplishment. From start to finish, all Americans assumed a resolute attitude that made the impossible routine. When Americans know their cause is just and their goal is clear, they are intrepid. The American values embedded in the soldiers led to the professionalism that was the fundamental difference between the two opposing forces and the deciding factor. In the future, the Army must continue to maintain a quality that builds on the positive qualities of the American character. Our soldiers will always be the strength of our Army.

APPENDIX A

Glossary

A/13 FA	A Battery, 13th Field Artillery
A/3 Engr	A Company, 3d Engineer Battalion
ACE	armored combat engineer
ACR	armored cavalry regiment
ADA	air defense artillery
ADC(M)	assistant division commander (maneuver)
ADC(S)	assistant division commander (support)
ALOC	administrative and logistics operations center
AO	area of operations
A/S3	battle captains
BP	battle position
BSA	brigade support area
C3	command, control, and communications
C/124 MI	C Company, 124th Military Intelligence Battalion
CENTCOM	Central Command
CEOI	Communications-Electronics Operation Instructions
CESO	communications and electronics support officer
CG	commanding general
CP	command post
CRP	combat reconnaissance patrol
CSM	Command Sergeant Major
CSS	combat service support
CUCV	combat utility cargo vehicle
D/4 Cav	D Troop, 4th Cavalry
DCO	deputy commander
DISCOM	division support command
DMZ	demilitarized zone

DSA	division support area
DTAC	division tactical command post (forward command post)
EPW	enemy prisoner of war
FARP	forward area refuel point
FM	frequency modulation
FRAGO	fragmentary order
FSB	forward support battalion
FSCL	fire support coordination line
FSE	forward security element
FSO	fire support officer
G-day	Ground war-day (code name given to the day the ground war would begin)
GPS	global positioning system
H-hour	planned attack time
HEMTT	heavy expanded mobility tactical truck (two types: fuel and cargo)
HET	heavy equipment transporter
HHT	headquarters and headquarters troop
HMMWV	high-mobility multipurpose wheeled vehicle
ITV	improved TOW vehicle
LD	line of departure
LO	liaison officer
MAPEX	map exercise
MEDEVAC	medical evacuation
METT-T	mission, enemy, terrain, troops, and time available
MLRS	multiple-launch rocket system
MOPP	mission-oriented protection posture

MP	military police
MRE	meal, ready to eat
MSB	main support battalion
NCO	noncommissioned officer
NCOIC	noncommissioned officer in charge
NLT	not later than
NTC	National Training Center
Obj	objective
OP	observation post
OPCON	operational control
OPFOR	opposing forces
OPORD	operation order
PIR	priority information requests
PL	phase line
PSYOP	psychological operations
PX	post exchange
R&S	reconnaissance and security
RATT	radio and teletype
REDCON	readiness condition
RFL	restrictive firing line
S1	adjutant
S2	intelligence and security officer
S3	operations officer
S4	logistics and supply officer
SCO	squadron commander
SIB	separate infantry brigade
SITREP	situation report
SMO	squadron maintenance officer
SXO	squadron executive officer

TAA	tactical assembly area
TAC CP	tactical command post
TACSAT	tactical satellite
TEWT	tactical exercise without troops
TF	task force
TF Air Cav	Task Force Air Cavalry
TOC	tactical operations center
TOCEX	tactical operations center exercise
TOE	table of organization and equipment
TOW	tube-launched, optically tracked, wire guided
197 SIB	197th separate infantry brigade
2-4 Cav	2d Squadron, 4th Cavalry Regiment
2-9 Cav	2d Squadron, 9th Cavalry Regiment
3-15 Inf	3d Battalion, 15th Infantry Regiment
24 ID(M)	24th Infantry Division (Mechanized)
UHF	ultra high frequency
UMCP	unit maintenance collection point
VHF	very high frequency

APPENDIX B

Key Personnel, 24th Infantry Division (Mechanized)

Commanding General
Major General Barry R. McCaffrey

Assistant Division Commander (Maneuver)
Brigadier General James T. Scott

Assistant Division Commander (Support)
Brigadier General Joe N. Frazar III

Command Sergeant Major
Sergeant Major James D. Randolph

Task Force 2d Squadron, 4th Cavalry Regiment (Operations Desert Shield and Storm), 7 August 1990-23 March 1991

Squadron Commander
Lieutenant Colonel Glynn Pope	7 Aug. 1990-22 Jan. 1991
Major (P) Louis Gelling Jr.	23-28 Jan. 1991
Lieutenant Colonel Thomas J. Leney	29 Jan. 1991-23 Mar. 1991

Command Sergeant Major
Sergeant Major Joseph Terian	7 Aug. 1990-15 Oct. 1990
Sergeant Major Jean L. Soucy	15 Nov. 1990-23 Mar. 1991

Deputy Squadron Commander
Major (P) Louis Gelling Jr.	25 Dec. 1990-23 Mar. 1991

Executive Officer
Major L. Clay Edwards	7 Aug. 1990-18 Jan. 1991
Major Joseph C. Barto III	2 Feb. 1991-23 Mar. 1991

Adjutant (S1)
Captain David Andersen
NCOIC:
Staff Sergeant David Morris	7 Aug. 1990-15 Dec. 1990
Sergeant First Class James Hill	16 Dec. 1990-23 Mar. 1991

Intelligence and Security (S2)
Captain Lee Wimbish	7 Aug. 1990-1 Feb. 1991
Captain Karl Buchanan	1 Feb. 1991-23 Mar. 1991
NCOIC:
Sergeant First Class Phillip Townsend	7 Aug. 1990-23 Mar. 1991

Battlefield Information Coordinator
First Lieutenant Brian Edholm   7 Aug.-23 Mar. 1991

Operations (S3)
Major Gregory Stone   7 Aug. 1990-2 Feb. 1991
Captain Peter Utley   3 Feb. 1991-23 Mar. 1991
NCOIC:
    Master Sergeant McDonald   7 Aug. 1990-21 Feb. 1991
    Master Sergeant (P) Bernard Cabrerra   22 Feb.1991-23 Mar. 1991

Battle Captains (A/S3)
Captain Peter Utley (S3 Air)   7 Aug. 1990-2 Feb. 1991
Captain Jeffrey Bierl   3 Feb. 1991-23 Mar. 1991
Captain Bruce Weatherspoon   7 Aug. 1990-30 Jan. 1991
Captain Rans Black (S3 Air)   31 Jan. 1991-23 Mar. 1991

Fire Support Officer
Captain Melvin Murray   7 Aug. 1990-2 Dec. 1990
Captain Clifford Hefner   2 Dec. 1990-23 Mar. 1991
NCOIC:
    Sergeant First Class Joseph Torres   7 Aug. 1990-23 Mar. 1991

Flight Operations Officer
Captain Daniel Miller   2 Dec. 1990-22 Feb. 1991

Chemical Officer
Second Lieutenant Michael Fite
NCOIC:
    Sergeant First Class Kinney   7 Aug. 1990-23 Mar. 1991

Logistics and Supply Officer (S4)
Captain Gordon Harrison   7 Aug. 1990-23 Mar. 1991
NCOIC:
    Sergeant First Class Roberto Santos   7 Aug. 1990-23 Mar. 1991

Support Platoon Leader
First Lieutenant Robert Hamilton   7 Aug. 1990-23 Mar. 1991
Support platoon sergeant:
    Staff Sergeant Daniel Allen   7 Aug.1990-23 Mar. 1991

Squadron Maintenance Officer
Captain Jeffrey Kelley   7 Aug. 1990-23 Mar. 1991
Squadron maintenance technician:
   Chief Warrant Officer Curlen Richardson   7 Aug. 1990-23 Mar. 1991
NCOIC:
   Master Sergeant James Stewart   7 Aug. 1990-23 Mar. 1991

Signal Officer
Captain Steven Noel
NCOIC:
   Sergeant First Class Kenneth Brown

Squadron Surgeon
Captain (Dr.) Robert Kazragis   7 Aug. 1990-23 Mar. 1991

Squadron Medical Platoon Leader
Second Lieutenant Wayne White   3 Feb. 1991-23 Mar. 1991

Physician's Assistant
Chief Warrant Officer Martin Laxson   7 Aug. 1990-23 Mar. 1991

Headquarters and Headquarters Troop

Commander
Captain Amador L. Cano Jr.   31 May 1990-20 Aug. 1991

Executive Officer
First Lieutenant Scott Mason   7 Aug. 1990-15 Sept. 1990
First Lieutenant Brian Hann   16 Sept. 1990-23 Mar. 1991
First sergeant:
   First Sergeant Irtenkauff   7 Aug. 1990-23 Mar. 1991
Mess sergeant:
   Sergeant First Class Stewart   7 Aug. 1990-23 Mar. 1991

Troop A, 2d Squadron, 4th Cavalry Regiment

Commander
Captain David Gallup   7 Aug. 1990-23 Mar. 1991

Executive Officer
First Lieutenant Brian Hann   7 Aug. 1990-15 Sept. 1990
First Lieutenant John Roddy   16 Sept. 1990-23 Mar. 1991

First Sergeant
First Sergeant Charles O. Hill   7 Aug. 1990-23 Mar. 1991

1st Platoon Leader

Second Lieutenant James Hundley	7 Aug. 1990-30 Jan. 1991
Sergeant First Class Robert Soto	31 Jan. 1991-21 Feb. 1991
First Lieutenant Lim Ko	22 Feb. 1991-23 Mar. 1991

1st Platoon Sergeant Sergeant

First Class Robert Soto	7 Aug. 1990-31 Jan. 1991
Sergeant First Class Johnson	1 Feb. 1991-23 Mar. 1991

2d Platoon Leader

First Lieutenant Scott Mason	7 Aug. 1990-23 Mar. 1991

2d Platoon Sergeant

Sergeant First Class Bringle	7 Aug. 1990-23 Mar. 1991

3d Platoon Leader

Second Lieutenant David Holcombe	7 Aug. 1990-23 Mar. 1991

3d Platoon Sergeant

Sergeant First Class Bell	7 Aug. 1990-23 Mar. 1991

Fire Support Officer

Second Lieutenant Timothy Pickles	7 Aug. 1990-23 Mar. 1991
NCOIC:	
Sergeant Halligan	7 Aug. 1990-23 Mar. 1991
Mortar section sergeant:	
Staff Sergeant Blake	7 Aug. 1990-23 Mar. 1991

Troop D, 4th Cavalry, 197th Brigade

Commander
Captain Thomas Dimassimmo

Executive Officer
First Lieutenant John Hirst

First Sergeant
Sergeant First Class Fowler

1st Platoon Leader
Second Lieutenant Harris

1st Platoon Sergeant
Sergeant First Class Broadhurst

2d Platoon Leader
Second Lieutenant Hupp

2d Platoon Sergeant
Sergeant First Class Nelms

3d Platoon Leader
Second Lieutenant Segars

3d Platoon Sergeant
Sergeant First Class McGhee

4th Platoon Leader
Second Lieutenant Davidson

4th Platoon Sergeant
Sergeant First Class Purdue

Fire Support Officer
First Lieutenant Terry Ivester

Company D, 3d Battalion, 69th Armor

Commander
Captain Michael Foley

Executive Officer
First Lieutenant Gerard Cribb

First Sergeant
First Sergeant Jay Lienhard

1st Platoon Leader
First Lieutenant Barry Householder

2d Platoon Leader
Second Lieutenant Antony Castagno

3d Platoon Leader
Second Lieutenant William Kilkenny

Company A, 3d Engineer Battalion

Commander
Captain Steve Haag

Executive Officer
First Lieutenant James Hardison

First Sergeant
First Sergeant Roy Owens

1st Platoon Leader
First Lieutenant Chris Papaiounnou

2d Platoon Leader
Second Lieutenant Tracy Turner

3d Platoon Leader
Second Lieutenant John Boldue

4th Platoon Leader
First Lieutenant Doug Zanger

A Battery, 13th Field Artillery (MLRS)

Commander
Captain William Norton

Executive Officer
First Lieutenant William Doyle

First Sergeant
First Sergeant Kenneth Porter

NOTES

1. John K. Herr and Edward S. Wallace, T*he Story of the U.S. Cavalry* (Boston, MA:Little, Brown, and Co., 1953). [Page 1]

2. Excerpts from the lineage and honors of the 2d Squadron, 4th Cavalry. [Page 2]

3. Interviews with Command Sergeant Major Jean Soucy and Master Sergeant (P) Bernard Cabrerra. Between these two soldiers, they had been assigned as senior NCOs in both 2-9 Cav and 2-4 Cav from 1982 to 1992. [Page 3]

4. In peacetime, the squadron's second ground cavalry troop, B Troop, was found in the Georgia National Guard as part of the "round-out" brigade. Only two of the three maneuver brigades of the 24th Infantry Division (Mechanized) were in the Active Component. [Page 5]

5. Interviews and an essay submitted by Captain Peter Utley, who commanded A Troop for two years prior to the Persian Gulf deployment and served as the assistant S3 and S3 of the squadron throughout Operations Desert Shield and Storm. [Page 9]

6. Ibid. [Page 14]

7. The discussion of the organization for combat is a synopsis of the squadron's tactical standard operating procedures as modified to the situation and implemented during the campaign. [Page 17]

8. Interview with Major (P) Louis Gelling Jr. [Page 17]

9. The discussion of the combat service support organization for combat is a synopsis of the squadron's tactical standard operating procedures as modified to the situation and implemented during the campaign. [Page 19]

10. Interview with Lieutenant Colonel Thomas J. Leney as he recounted his journey from Washington, D.C., to Saudi Arabia. [Page 23]

11. Interview and report of Captain David Gallup, Commander, A Troop, 2-4 Cav. [Page 38]

12. Interview with Lieutenant Colonel Thomas J. Leney, who was present during the refugee evacuation exercise. [Page 38]

13. Interview with Command Sergeant Major Soucy, who was the NCO in charge of the cavalry stables operation. [Page 39]

14. *Soviet Army Equipment, Organization, and Operations* (Fort Leavenworth, KS: Combined Arms and Services Staff School), 346. [Page 55]

15. Interviews with Lieutenant Colonel Leney and Captain Gallup, who executed the reconnaissance. Leney was present in the TAC CP and controlled this operation because the TF's main CP was out of FM radio range. [Page 58]

16. Report rendered to the executive officer by First Lieutenant Brian Edholm, who conducted the interrogation of these Iraqi prisoners of war. [Page 71]

17. Interview with Major Gelling, who executed the mission to obtain the fuel resupply assets. [Page 72]

18. Interview with Lieutenant Colonel Leney, who personally observed and controlled this action. [Page 86]

19. Interview with First Lieutenant John Roddy, Executive Officer of A Troop, who was present at the scene. [Page 95]

20. The division command post issued the guidance on the categorizing and treatment of EPWs and refugees. [Page 96]

21. Interview with Chief Warrant Officer Laxson, squadron physician's assistant. [Page 96]

22. Interview with Lieutenant Colonel Leney, who received the guidance directly from the commanding general. [Page 101]

23. Interview with Major Gelling, who was in charge of the entire recovery operation in the bog. [Page 106]

24. Interview with Lieutenant Colonel Leney and Staff Sergeant James Gill, NCO in charge of the TAC CP. [Page 109]

25. Battle damage assessment report compiled by the squadron S2, Captain Karl Buchanan, and submitted to division upon completion of the mission. [Page 115]

26. Jason K. Kamiya, *A History of the 24th Mechanized Infantry Division Combat Team During Operation Desert Storm,* published by the 24th Infantry Division (Mechanized), p. 33. Major Kamiya was also the primary author of the Battle Summary found in the "Victory Book," which was published as a record of the campaign by Josten's Publishing Company for the 24th ID(M) combat team. [Page 117]

PICTURES

Please Visit Your Website and Participate!

As a supplement to the 25th Anniversary Edition, a website forum has been created where troopers, their families, and anyone associated with this historical event and time, can have a place to share their stories and pictures. Another edition to this book may result, if there is enough participation, to include these stories and pictures.

We highly encourage Desert Storm veterans to view the website, the video, and to participate through the forum.

The website is: www.taskforce24cav.com

Copies of this book can be purchased through **www.Lulu.com**. Search for *Task Force 2/4 Cav "First In, Last Out"*. No profit is made from publishing.

EDITORS POSTSCRIPT & SUMMATION

The author graciously invited us to write a few words about our involvement with the book and the story of how this re-publication came into being.

Tambra McCowen:

Having never been in the military or around it, (other than marrying a veteran who tells wonderful stories about his experiences), I had no idea what it truly means to be in the military with it's discipline, commands, and leadership. Reading this book clarified some things regarding my husband and why he does things a certain way.

As I typed, formatted, edited, and proofread this edition, I wondered many things. How can huge, heavy vehicles be pulled out of the bog and on such a tight timeline? Who made that "Christmas tree held up by reindeer" (and out of what) that is pictured? What was it like to drive through the blowing sand or heavy rain and stay on track? Who had the presence of mind and the decency to cover the dead Iraqi soldiers on Highway 8? Joe got knocked down by a "flying tent", which isn't funny, but I laughed when he imagined what could have been said by the Army to his wife. I'm sure many soldiers who were there have stories they have shared with others and those stories should be in here.

There are great sub-stories within the main story and the book is almost demanding that others recount their participation to compliment Joe Barto's excellent macro-overview from the command level to fill in gaps. He has wanted wholeheartedly for those involved in TF 2-4 Cav to add their stories and pictures to the original version. My husband created a website forum (see page 142 for the address) where veterans can easily add them or email them to be shared. If you don't type, someone you know does. If not, please write your stories and email them through the website's link. If enough people share their stories, we can create another, more complete edition!

It has been a pleasure to help get this ready for publication. My husband and I have donated copies to the local library and requested they be made available to the public. This book is for everyone, not just those who are or have been in the Army. Their families (grandchildren) and neighbors and all those who are protected by soldiers, will enjoy this book and get an insight into those who serve and risk their lives for their country. They will gain perspectives that they, otherwise, could not get.

We also had fun creating a video to honor 2-4 Cav that is on the website! I hope you enjoy it.

Bill McCowen:

January 1981, I am laying in a hospital bed in the ICU at Ireland Army Hospital, Ft. Knox, KY. An Army Doctor is trying to convince me, unsuccessfully, to have my ruptured spleen and my gall bladder removed and they have yet to look at my back, which I am certain is broken. On top of trying to convince me to give up my organs, he explained that I will most likely be medically discharged from the Army and lose my career along with my organs. This all as a result of a 13 foot, full gainer belly-flop off the turret of an M60A3 tank while on a firing range.

I remember I was more afraid of being sent back home, disabled, to Podunk U.S.A., than I was about my health. That fear drove me to get out of that bed that night and start crawling. I found that I couldn't walk. By the next night I was stumbling. In three days I walked out of that hospital after blackballing the Doctor. I stank like a pig because they just threw my field fatigues into a trash bag where they sat, fermenting in all of the bile, vomit, and blood from my accident.

Once I arrived back to my unit's orderly room after a jeep ride, I knew I was in trouble. I had never felt so much pain in my life, but there was no way I was going back to that hospital. My future was uncertain. Fortunately, my Commanding Officer was there and he ushered me into his office and welcomed me back. After some small talk, he shared with me a story about a friend who had died at West Point from a ruptured spleen and stated that he was glad that I was ok. Then he remembered he had 10,000 things to do in running his unit and dismissed me. On the way to the door, after the customary salute, he walked over to me before I could get out the door and laid a hand on my shoulder and stopped me. I will never forget what he said to me and how that made me feel.

He looked me in the eye and told me straight-up that I was strong, though I may not feel like it right now, and the whole command supported me fully to help me get back to full duty as soon as possible and that he believed in me and I would fully recover. For good measure, he reiterated that "I am strong. I can overcome this." He believed in me.

That was all I needed to hear. I stood tall and marched myself the 1/4 mile to my barracks with my lower body numb and tears of pain running off my cheeks. I still had not told anyone about my back. Thirty days later, I was back on full duty. To this day, my back is chronically broken and hurts, but I still have all my organs and have had a full life.

Now fast forward 37 years later. Here I am writing part of an Editors Afterword for his book's 25th Anniversary Edition for re-publication. This is where this little story gets strange.

I had not seen or talked to Joe Barto since a chance encounter when he left squadron headquarters where he was the outgoing Commander of Bravo Troop in 3/12 Cav, 3rd AD in Germany in 1984.

Late summer of 2017, while I was battling a potentially life threatening illness coupled with a life of accumulated injuries, my wife Googled his name while I reminisced about my time at Fort Knox. I was probably talking about what he had said to me after I escaped the hospital and how that had helped me through the years whenever injured and in pain.

The next thing I know, I'm sending him an email communicating to him straight-up what a major, positive impact he had on my life. Not only for believing in me enough to make me a tank commander at age 17, but also that he helped me stand tall during the most painful and frightening time of my young life. How he and my platoon sergeant, Sergeant Powell, tried to convince me to get into West Point and ultimately how that effected me for life. These simple, yet profound acts of leadership at the right time, right place, and for the right reason, steered my course from then on.

He responded to my email and a couple phone calls ensued. I did not tell him how bad I was physically and mentally. It just felt good to reconnect. When he confided in me that he had survived, not once but twice, a life threatening illness, something in me kind of snapped.

A weird de-ja-vue ensued along with a huge dose of inspiration and motivation. Once again, through all the fear and physical pain I was experiencing, I stood up tall and began to march forward, with no excuses, ever so slowly.

This re-publication is the result of these chance encounters and Joe's (and our) wish to get the book re-published. Not only am I healthy again, despite my injuries, I am mentally getting myself back in the game of life, where just six short months before things were very uncertain for my wife and I.

As one may readily discern, my wife, Tambra, plays a major part in this story as well. All the credit for this project being completed goes to her, as well as to Joe's leadership and skill. He has authored a world class book. This book and the story is for all the veterans of TF 2-4 Cav. You are all such an inspiration to my wife and I and since it touches us so deeply, we know it will others. This is basically our story and the reason for our involvement with *Task Force 2-4 Cav -"First In Last Out"*.

I must be very clear on something. I need to impress upon the reader what this book and "Cav Troopers" are all about and the power that resolute, professional leadership can inspire in all of us. I attribute any and all of my professional achievements to my chain of command in C-3-1 while at Ft. Knox, KY (1980-81). I was able to continue in life with a crooked body because my leaders let me know that they believed in me and re-enforced my strengths as a human being.

So if any of you Veterans of TF 2/4 Cav are out there reading this, I implore you to get your stories on the Task Force 2/4 website forum and with enough of them, you can take this still incomplete book further. Incomplete because there are a thousand of these stories out there. They just need to be written down. If I can do it, so can you. I especially want to hear about (and from) the Stars and Stripes reporter.

Either way, we are proud of you. All of this is to honor you. From my unit to yours, Strength and Honor - Prepared and Loyal.